Elias Davidson Kennedy

History of the Descendants of William Kennedy and His Wife Mary or Marian Henderson

From 1730 to 1880, carried down by numbers. To which is added the

meaning of the name Kennedy, with some facts connected with their

history in Scotland and Ireland

Elias Davidson Kennedy

History of the Descendants of William Kennedy and His Wife Mary or Marian Henderson
From 1730 to 1880, carried down by numbers. To which is added the meaning of the name Kennedy, with some facts connected with their history in Scotland and Ireland

ISBN/EAN: 9783337323301

Printed in Europe, USA, Canada, Australia, Japan

Cover: Foto ©ninafisch / pixelio.de

More available books at **www.hansebooks.com**

HISTORY

OF

THE DESCENDANTS

OF

WILLIAM KENNEDY AND HIS WIFE MARY OR MARIAN HENDERSON,

FROM 1730 TO 1880, CARRIED DOWN BY NUMBERS.

TO WHICH IS ADDED

THE MEANING OF THE NAME KENNEDY, WITH SOME FACTS CONNECTED WITH THEIR HISTORY IN SCOTLAND AND IRELAND.

COMPILED BY

ELIAS DAVIDSON KENNEDY,

FOR PRIVATE USE.

PHILADELPHIA:
PRESS OF HENRY B. ASHMEAD,
Nos. 1102 AND 1104 SANSOM STREET.
1881.

PREFACE.

NOTWITHSTANDING all the care that has been spent on the preparation of this work, the Author cannot say that he is satisfied. Though he has done all in his power to collect information relating to the history of each person mentioned, the book must appear to his readers, as it appears to himself, defective in execution and meagre in detail. But had he made perfection his standard it would never have been printed. It is now given to the members of the Kennedy family, in the hope that it may preserve a lively interest in their past history.

The original design was to collect the names of the descendants of William Kennedy and his wife Mary Henderson—she was sometimes called Marian—from the time of their settlement in Bucks County, in 1730, with the view of placing the manuscript in some library, for safe keeping and future reference; but it has been thought best to accede to the request of many members of the family, to have it published for their use.

With the view of keeping the work within reasonable size, and in order to make it practically useful, it has been found necessary to mention only, and that in a very brief way, the main or essential facts in each person's history, viz., the birth, marriage, number of children, profession or business, religion, politics, and residence. This rule has been varied from, in a few instances, in order to introduce the biography of some men of historic interest. It is regretted that, in some instances, correspondents have furnished only the names of the members of their family, without any connecting history.

KEY.

(*) Refers to the descriptive part.

(†) Extinct.

The dark figures are used to bring the name down, so as to put the children together.

No.	NAME.	BIRTH. Date and Place.	DEATH. Date and Place.	MARRIAGE. Date and Place.	TO WHOM MARRIED.	REMARKS.
*A	Robert Kennedy,	(North Ireland 1693. . .)	March 26, 1776,	. . .	Mary,	This family not traced. See description.
*1	William Kennedy,	(North Ireland Londonderry,)	1777 or 1778,	. . .	Mary Henderson. Sometimes called by the Scotch name Marian.	Presbyterian.
	Second Generation.					
†2	Thomas Kennedy,	1729, (Bucks Co., Pa.,)	Jan. 24, 1794,	. . .	Janet,	No issue.
‡3	James Kennedy,	1730, . . .	October 7, 1799,	1761,	(1 w. Jane Maxwell, / 2 w. Jane Macanly,)	Twelve children.
4	Robert Kennedy,	March 28, 1733,	April 13, 1812,	1764,	Elizabeth Hearrie,	No issue.
†5	John Kennedy,	. . .	. . .	. . .	Unmarried.	Buried, Greenwich, N. J.
†6	Lucy Kennedy,	. . .	. . .	. . .	William Macauly,	
7	Mary Kennedy,	. . .	Easton,	. . .	Col. Arthur Erwin. 2d wife.	No issue.
†8	Rebecca Jane Kennedy,	. . .	. . .	. . .	Unmarried.	
	Third Generation.					
3	JAMES and JANE MAXWELL KENNEDY.					
9	Ann Kennedy,	1762,	. . .	. . .	Phineas Barber.	(Farmer, Stewartsville, N. J. Federalist and Whig; Presbyterian.
10	Thomas Kennedy,	1764,	1847,	. . .	Margaret Stewart,	Judge; Dem.; Elder Presb. Church.
*11	William Kennedy,	1766,	1850,	. . .	Sarah Stewart.	Presbyterian; Democrat.
12	John Kennedy,	1768,	Died young, April 1791,	. . .	Elizabeth Linn,	
†13	Lucy Kennedy,	1770,				
14	Jane Kennedy,	1772,		. . .	Samuel Kennedy,	Warren, O.
15	Elizabeth Kennedy,	1774,	July 24, 1847,	. . .	(1 h. John Young, / 2 h. William Moorhead,)	Soon after Mrs. Moorhead lost her second husband she returned, with her six small children, to Moorhead's Ferry, and in the absence of church privileges, she offered her house to the Methodists for itinerant preaching, and soon thereafter joined that church. At this time both the Presbyterian and Methodist Churches have their ministerial rolls honored by several of her descendants.

No.	NAME.	BIRTH, Date and Place.	DEATH, Date and Place.	MARRIAGE, Date and Place.	TO WHOM MARRIED.	REMARKS.
16	James Kennedy,	1776,			Elizabeth Maxwell,	Presbyterian; Farmer; Federalist. Lancaster Co., Pa.
*17	Robert Kennedy,	July 4, 1778,	October 31, 1843,	{ Feb. 17, 1801, June 5, 1806,	1 w. Jane Herron, 2 w. Mary Davidson,	Presb. Preacher; Federalist; Whig. Welsh Run, Franklin Co., Pa.
18	Mary Kennedy,	1780,			John Logan.	
19	Nameless.					
20	Maxwell Kennedy,	1782,	1844,		Margaret Maxwell,	Whig; Farmer; Presb.; Member of Legislature. (iap, Lancaster Co., Pa.
4	Robert and Elizabeth Heanie Kensedy.					
†21	John Kennedy,	June 6, 1765,	Died young.			
22	Mary Ann Kennedy,	Jan. 30, 1767,			John R. Reading.	
23	Jane Kennedy,	Jan. 14, 1769,			Daniel Reading.	
†24	Hannah Cook Kennedy,	Jan. 17, 1774,				
†25	Enoch Kennedy,	Nov. 14, 1776,	Dead. No issue.		Miss Williamson.	Woodbury, N. J.
26	Elizabeth Kennedy,	May 16, 1782,			James Maduck, 1st wife, 2d wife, James Maduck,	Woodbury, N. J.
27	Keturah Cook Kennedy,	Oct. 2, 1792,				
28	Robert Heanie Kennedy,	Aug. 12, 1787,	Jan. 29, 1859,	{ Nov. 17, 1813, May 3, 1837,	1 w. Miriam Kay, 2 w. Sally Ann Reader,	Bloomsburg, N. J., Capitalist.
29	Esther Heanie Kennedy,	March 25, 1785,			John Killie,	Mt. Holly, N. J.
7	Arthur and Mary Kensedy Erwin.					
30	Samuel Erwin,				Rachel Hickman.	
†31	Frank Erwin,				Unmarried.	
†32	Arthur Erwin,				Unmarried.	Doctor. — Easton, Pa.
†33	John Erwin,				Dr. McKeen,	Easton, Pa.
34	Rebecca Erwin,				Dr. John Cooper,	
35	Mary Erwin,					
9	Phineas and Ann Kensedy Barber.					
†36	James Barber,	April 19, 1780,	Jan. 11, 1838,		Polly Tilghman. No issue.	Presbyterian; Farmer; Democrat.
37	Mary Barber,	Aug. 22, 1781,	Nov. 8, 1847,	March 4, 1804,	William Marr,	Presb.; Farmer. Northumberland Co., Pa.
†38	Lillie Barber,		Died in infancy.			

7

No.	NAME	BIRTH, Date and Place	DEATH, Date and Place	MARRIAGE, Date and Place	TO WHOM MARRIED.	REMARKS.
39	John Barber,	Jan. 15, 1784,	. . .	. . .	Hannah Donaldson,	Presbyterian; Farmer. Canada.
40	Jane Barber,	Aug. 24, 1785,	. . .	. . .	Robert McCurley,.	Presbyterian; Farmer; Whig. Union Co., Pa.
41	Thomas K. Barber,	Sept. 15, 1787,	. . .	. . .	Mary Henderson..	Presbyterian; Farmer; Democrat. Columbia Co., Pa.
42	Nancy Barber,	July 13, 1790,	Dec. 12, 1825,	Aug. 6, 1815,	Samuel Henderson,	Democrat; Presbyterian; Farmer. Union Co., Pa.
43	William Barber,	. . .	Died in infancy.			
44	William Barber,	May 9, 1795,	Sept. 28, 1871,	Feb. 2, 1819, / Jan. 29, 1851,	1 w. Margaret Clyde, / 2 w. Elizabeth Adams,	Presbyterian; Quaker; Methodist; Dem.; Farmer and Merchant. Mansfield, Ohio. Farmer; Presb.; Democrat.
45	Elizabeth Barber,	Jan. 18, 1797,			Robert Moorhead,	Presb. Preacher. Jersey Shore, Pa. Republican.
46	Daniel M. Barber,	March 6, 1800,	Oct. 30, 1865,	1821, / 1822,	1 w. Sarah Moorhead, / 2 w. Elizabeth Sharron, / 1 h. John McCollum, / 2 h. Peter Weigle.	Pres.; Farmer; Dem. Columbia, Pa.
47	Sallie Barber,	Jan. 19, 1802,				
†48	Peggy Barber,	May 10, 1804,	1848,		Wm. H. Sullivan. No issue.	
49	Jesse Barber,	May 10, 1804,			Mary Funston,	Presbyterian; Farmer.
†50	Nameless.					
†51	Robert Barber,	Sept. 23, 1806.			Unmarried.	
10	THOMAS and MARGARET STEWART KENNEDY.					
52	James Kennedy,	May 19, 1790.	April 8, 1842,	March 27, 1810,	Jane Clyde,.	Elder Presb. Church; Farmer; Dem. Northumberland Co., Pa.
53	Sarah Kennedy,				John Kerr.	Warren Co., N. J.
54	Jane Kennedy,				Alexander Innes,	Warren Co., N. J.
55	Margaret Kennedy,				Adam D. Runkle,	
†56	Ann Kennedy.					
57	Elizabeth Kennedy,				George Barber,	Warren Co., N. J.
58	Robert S. Kennedy,				Catharine Strader,	Judge; Republican; Presb. Elder; Farmer. Stewartsville, N. J.
†59	Mary Kennedy.					
11	WILLIAM and SARAH STEWART KENNEDY.					
†60	Robert Stewart Kennedy,	May 5, 1791,			Died young.	No family.
†61	Jane Kennedy,				Joseph Kerr.	

No.	NAME.	BIRTH, Date and Place.	DEATH, Date and Place.	MARRIAGE, Date and Place.	TO WHOM MARRIED.	REMARKS.
62	James J. Kennedy,	July 14, 1793,	Nov. 9, 1865,	Jan. 28, 1819,	Margaret Cowell,	Judge; Democrat; Presbyterian. Removed from Warren Co., N.J., to Chambersburg, Pa., 1839. Was a prominent agriculturist.
63	Wm. Maxwell Kennedy,	Sept. 23, 1795,	Sept. 25, 1839,	Feb. 17, 1825,	Maria Kerr,	Democrat; Presbyterian; Farmer. Warren Co., N.J.
64	Stewart Kennedy,	Sept. 17, 1798,	March 1, 1852,	May 3, 1821,	Ann Ferguson,	Doctor; Democrat; Elder Presb. Church. Chambersburg, Pa. A gentleman highly esteemed.
†65	Thomas Kennedy,	Oct. 7, 1800,	Oct. 4, 1827,	·	Jane Corilla Green,	Presb. Preacher; Teacher. One child. Family extinct.
66	Phineas B. Kennedy,	Oct. 28, 1802,	·	Sept. 20, 1825,	Priscilla Kerr,	Lawyer; Democrat; Elder Presb. Church. Belvidere, N.J.
67	Sallie Kennedy,	Oct. 21, 1804,	June 26, 1843,	·	George S. Green, 1st wife.	Elder Presb. Church; Merchant; Republican. Trenton, N.J.
12	JOHN and ELIZABETH LINN KENNEDY.					
68	Jane Maxwell Kennedy,	·	·	·	Michael Christian.	Farmer; Democrat; Presbyterian.
69	James Kennedy,	·	·	·	Mary McWilliams,	Republican; Presbyterian.
70	Thomas Kennedy,	·	·	·	Sarah Sloan,	
71	Katharine Kennedy,	·	·	·	Not married.	
72	John Kennedy,	·	Died young.	·		
73	Margaret Kennedy,	·	Died young.	·		
74	Robert Kennedy,	·	·	·	Margaret Johnston,	Democrat; Presbyterian. Indiana.
14	SAMUEL and JANE KENNEDY.					
75	Robt. Montgomery Kennedy	April 6, 1792,	·	·	Mary Battles,	Howland Co., O. Farmer.
76	Jane Maxwell Kennedy,	June 16, 1794,	·	·	David B. King,	Howland Co., O. Farmer.
77	Nancy Kennedy,	Feb. 26, 1797.	·	·	Samuel King,	Farmer. Howland Co., O.
78	Mary Barber Kennedy,	Feb. 22, 1801.	1860,	1820,	William King,	Howland Township, O. Presb.; Whig; Republican; Farmer.
79	Thomas Kennedy,	April 18, 1810,	·	May 11, 1837,	Phebe Casterline,	Republican; United Brethren. Courtland, O.
80	William B. Kennedy,	Sept. 21, 1812,	·	Sept. 24, 1857,	Eliza Davis, granddaughter of Gen. Stark,	Farmer. Courtland, O.

No.	NAME.	BIRTH, DATE AND PLACE.	DEATH, DATE AND PLACE.	MARRIAGE, DATE AND PLACE.	TO WHOM MARRIED.	REMARKS.
81	James Kennedy,	July 30, 1805,		Nov. 10, 1831,	Alice Scott,	Farmer; Republican; Temp. "Do as wish to be done by." Howland, O.
82	Maxwell Kennedy,	July 30, 1807,		Dec. 5, 1833,	Eveline Doud,	United Brethren. Howland, O. Republican.
83	Tabitha Kennedy,	Jan. 7, 1804,	Aug. 23, 1871,	Jan. 7, 1864,	Samuel Kennedy,	Howland, O. Republican = Farmer.
84	Elizabeth Kennedy,	June 15, 1799,			Montgomery Anderson,	Howland, O.
85	Ann Kennedy,	Aug. 2, 1814,		March 24, 1836,	Morris J. Iddings, No issue.	Warren, O.
15	Elizabeth Kennedy. 1 h. John Young. 2 h. Wm. Moorhead.					
86	Jane Young,				Jacob Barr,	Member of Legislature.
87	Ellinor Young,	Jan. 1, 1801,	1826.		Unmarried.	
88	Maria Young,			1817,	William Cowlick,	
89	James Kennedy Moorhead,	Sept. 7, 1806,		Dec. 17, 1829,	Jane Logan,	Miller. Dauphin Co., Pa. Presb.; Congressman; Manufacturer, Pittsburg, Pa. Repub.
90	Joel Barlow Moorhead,	April 13, 1813,		Feb. 7, 1837,	Elizabeth Hirons,	Episcopalian; Manufacturer, Philadelphia. Republican.
91	Wm. Garroway Moorhead,	July 7, 1811,		Dec. 9, 1833,	1 w. Sarah Cooke, 2 w. Mrs. Cora-Badger.	Presb.; Banker; Dem. Philda.
92	Adeline Moorhead,		May 2, 1877,		Unmarried,	
93	Henry Clay Moorhead,	March 10, 1815,	April 15, 1861,		Unmarried,	Methodist.
94	Ann Moorhead,	Oct. 24, 1804,	Feb. 24, 1808,			Democrat; Lawyer; Methodist; Rheumatism. Philadelphia.
95	Eliza Moorhead,	March 15, 1802,	Aug. 29, 1858,	Jan. 24, 1826,	William Montgomery.	
16	James and Elizabeth Maxwell Kennedy.					
96	Jane Kennedy,				Unmarried.	
97	William S. Kennedy,				Margaret Byers,	Elder Presb.; Farmer; Republican. Lancaster Co., Pa.
98	Anna Maria Kennedy,				2 w. of George S. Green,	Trenton, N.J. Presb. Merchant.

No.	NAME.	BIRTH, Date and Place.	DEATH, Date and Place.	MARRIAGE, Date and Place.	TO WHOM MARRIED.	REMARKS.
17	ROBERT KENNEDY. 1 w. JANE HERRON. 2 w. MARY DAVIDSON.					
*99	John Herron Kennedy,	Nov. 11, 1801,	Dec. 15, 1840,	Feb. 15, 1827,	Harriet McCalmont,	Presb. Preacher; Professor: Whig. Canonsburg, Pa.
†100	Robert Kennedy,..	May 11, 1803,	Oct. 1, 1804.			
101	Nancy Davidson Kennedy,	April 18, 1807,	July 16, 1842,	April 22, 1834,	David Hunt,	Presbyterian; Dentist. Pittsburg. Whig.
†102	Eliza J. Herron Kennedy,	Feb. 5, 1811,	March 27, 1816.			
*103	James Maxwell Kennedy,	Feb. 24, 1809,	March 9, 1848,	Nov. 23, 1836,	Sibilla Stone Morris,	Presbyterian; Merchant. Philadelphia. Whig.
†104	Elias Davidson Kennedy,	May 30, 1815,	June 20, 1816.			
105	Mary Ann Kennedy, . .	Feb. 4, 1813,	Jan. 23, 1863,	March 5, 1840,	Lewis Martin, . .	Elder Presb. Church; Merchant; Whig; Repub. Delphi, Ind.
†106	Elizabeth Jane Kennedy,.	June 15, 1817,	Sept. 26, 1851,	July 20, 1847,	2 w. of Enoch Bowen,	One child; the family is extinct.
*107	Elias Davidson Kennedy,.	Dec. 27, 1819,		April 20, 1854,	Agnes Shields Clarke,	Presb.; Repub.; Merchant. Phila.
†108	Robt. Theophilus Kennedy,	Jan. 17, 1822,	Aug. 8, 1822,		Unmarried.	
†109	William Thomas Kennedy,	June 18, 1823,	Dec. 8, 1855,		Unmarried.	Merchant; Presb.; Repub. Phila.
†110	Henry Martyn Kennedy,.	Aug. 5, 1828,	Oct. 26, 1846,			
18	JOHN and MARY KENNEDY LOGAN.					
111	Jane Logan, ...				Jas. Kennedy Moorhead, traced in the Moorhead family.	
†112 113	Eliza Logan, ... James K. Logan, . .				Unmarried. Anna B. Finney,. . . . Mrs. Kennedy, who was a Miss Bryan, . .	Coal Merchant. Pittsburg, Pa. Merchant; Presb. Pittsburg, Pa.
114	John T. Logan, . . .					
115	Mary K. Logan, . . .	Sept. 7, 1811,		Nov. 16, 1827,	William H. Boyd, . .	Stewartsville, N. J.
20	MAXWELL and MARGARET MAXWELL KENNEDY.					
†116	Elinor Kennedy, . . .				Unmarried.	
117	Robert T. Kennedy,..				Charlotte Hambright, .	Merchant; Manuf.; Republican; Presbyterian. Pittsburg, Pa.

No.	NAME.	BIRTH, Date and Place.	DEATH, Date and Place.	MARRIAGE, Date and Place.	TO WHOM MARRIED.	REMARKS.
118	Winfield Scott Kennedy,	. . .	. . .	. . .	{ 1 w. Mary Malvina Slaymaker, 2 w. Esther J. Dickenson,	{ Farmer; Miller; Republican; Presbyterian. Lancaster Co., Pa.
119	Sylvester Kennedy, . . .	. . .	. . .	. . .	Martha A. Kinzer, . . .	{ Farmer; Republican; Presbyterian. Lancaster Co., Pa.
120	William Maxwell Kennedy, . . .	1809,	June, 1836,	. . .	Henrietta Bryan.	
121	Jane Kennedy, . . .			. . .	Andrew Byers.	
122	Nameless.					
123	"					
124	"					
125	"					
126	"					
22	JOHN R. and MARY ANN KENNEDY READING.					
127	Robert Kennedy Reading,	. . .	. . .	. . .	Maria Henrie, ...	New Jersey.
128	Theodocea Cook Reading,	. . .	. . .	. . .	{ 1 h. De Puy, . . . 2 h. Gen. Isaac G. Farley,	New Jersey. New Jersey,
†129	Eliza Kennedy Reading, . .	. . .	Died young.	. . .	Unmarried.	
†130	Daniel Reed Reading, . . .	. . .	. . .	. . .	Henry Disbro.	
131	Maria Reed Reading, . . .	. . .	. . .	. . .		
23	DANIEL and JANE KENNEDY READING.					
132	Elizabeth K. Reading, . . .	. . .	{ Deceased. No issue living. }	. . .	John Grandon.	
†132½	Daniel Kennedy Reading,	. . .	. . .	. . .	Mary Kennedy.	
133	Euphemia Reading, . . .	. . .	. . .	. . .	William Kennedy.	
26	JAMES MATLACK.					
27	1 w. ELIZABETH KENNEDY. 2 w. KETURAH C. KENNEDY.					
134	Hannah Cook Matlack, . .	. . .	. . .	. . .	Sylvester Scovel, . . .	{ Dr. of Divinity; Presb.; Prof. of Hanover College, Indiana.
135	Robert Kennedy Matlack,	. . .	. . .	. . .	Abbey Leaming, . . .	Woodbury, N. J.

No.	NAME.	BIRTH, Date and Place.	DEATH, Date and Place.	MARRIAGE, Date and Place.	TO WHOM MARRIED.	REMARKS.
136	Elizabeth Kennedy Matlack.	. . .	. . .	. . .	Abram Browning, . .	State Attorney: distinguished Lawyer: Episcopalian: Democrat. Camden, N. J.
28	Robert Heanne and Miriam Kay Kennedy.					
137	Heanrie Robert Kennedy, .	June 10, 1815,	. . .	. . .	Elizabeth LaGrange Frelinghuysen, daughter of Jno. Frelinghuysen,	Bloomsbury, N. J.
†138	Harriet Kay Kennedy, . .	Aug. 4, 1816,	Died in infancy.			
†139	Joseph Thorn Kennedy, .	July 11, 1817,	"			
†140	John Kennedy, . . .	Jan. 10, 1822,	"			
†141	Elizabeth Heanrie Kennedy.		"			
†142	Edmond Kennedy, . . .	1825, .	"			
†143	Franklin Kay Kennedy, .		"			
28	Of 2d Wife.					
†144	Enoch Kennedy, . . .		Died in infancy.			
†145	Frank Erwin Kennedy, .		"			
†146	Mary Kennedy, . . .		"			
29	John and Esther Heanrie Kennedy Killie.					
147	Eliza Kennedy Killie, . .					Mount Holly, N. J.
148	Robert Kennedy Killie, .					Mount Holly, N. J.
30	Samuel and Rachel Hickman Erwin.					
149	Samuel Erwin.					
150	Frank Erwin.					
151	Arthur Erwin.					
152	John Erwin.					
153	William Erwin.					
154	Charles Erwin.					
155	Mary Erwin.					
156	Eliza Erwin.					
157	Rachel Erwin.					

No.	NAME.	BIRTH, Date and Place.	DEATH, Date and Place.	MARRIAGE, Date and Place.	TO WHOM MARRIED.	REMARKS.
34	Dr. McKeen and Rebecca Erwin McKeen.					
158	Daughter,				Arthur Erwin,	Her cousin: eight or nine children.
35	Dr. John and Mary Erwin Cooper.					
159	John Cooper.					
160	Charlotte Cooper.					
161	Elizabeth Cooper.					
162	Sallie Ann Cooper.				Judge Randolph.	
37	William and Mary Barber Marr.					
163	Joseph Marr,	Mar. 11, 1806,			1 w. Miss Smith, 2 w. Miss Candor, 3 w. Mrs. Van Slyke,	Presbyterian Preacher. Harrisburg; 1st w., 5 child., 2d w., 1, 3d w., 5 child.; missionary to the Indians in Canada; 3d w. opened a successful female school in Milton, Pa., afterwards in Carondelet, Mo.
164	Phineas Barber Marr,	Jan. 20, 1808,	July 11, 1871,		Mary Graham,	Presb. Minister. Lewisburg, Pa.
165	Susanna Marr,	Nov. 16, 1809,	Jan. 20, 1871,		Phineas Barber,	Fingal, Canada.
166	Ann Marr,	Dec. 1, 1811,	June 11, 1841,		Samuel Bowman,	Canada.
†167	James B. Marr,	Feb. 26, 1814,			Unmarried.	
168	David Price Marr,	Feb. 12, 1816,	Sept. 2, 1861.	Dec. 17, 1839, Jan. 22, 1850,	1 w. Hetty L. Davis, 2 w. Harriet Matchin.	Presbyterian: Contractor. Milton, Pa.; Whig: Republican.
169	Margaret Marr,	July 15, 1820,			Dr. John McCollum.	Tiffin City, Ohio. No issue reported.
170	William H. Marr,	June 25, 1818,			Eliza Davis Baldwin.	Doctor. Lewisburg, Pa.
†171	Alem Kennedy Marr,	June 15, 1823,	Sept. 19, 1847.			
39	John and Hannah Donaldson Barber.					
172	Phineas Barber,	Feb. 18, 1812,		July 8, 1831,	Susan Marr,	Farmer. Fingal, Canada.
173	Jane Barber,	1814,		1833,	Leslie Pierce.	
†174	Maxfield Barber,	1817,			Not married,	Speculator. Waverly, Iowa.
175	Donaldson Barber,	1820,		1847,	Sarah Issent,	Farmer. Fingal, Canada.

No.	NAME.	BIRTH, Date and Place.	DEATH, Date and Place.	MARRIAGE, Date and Place.	TO WHOM MARRIED.	REMARKS.
40	ROBERT and JANE BARBER McCURLEY.					
†176	Joseph McCurley,				Unmarried.	
†177	Mary Ann McCurley,				Unmarried.	
†178	Roland McCurley,				Unmarried.	
179	James McCurley,				Married.	
41	THOMAS K. and MARY HENDERSON BARBER.					
†180	J. E. Barber,				Mary J. Marr,	No issue.
†181	Nancy Barber,				Unmarried.	
†182	Elizabeth Barber,				Unmarried.	
183	Joseph Barber,				Elizabeth Sproul.	
184	Jane Barber,				Married.	
†185	James Barber,				Unmarried.	
186	Daniel Barber,				Married.	
†187	Robert Barber,				Married.	Killed in the Rebel army.
188	Samuel H. Barber,					
42	SAMUEL and NANCY BARBER HENDERSON.					
†189	Ann B. Henderson,	Jan. 16, 1816,	Feb. 6, 1848.			
†190	Joseph Henderson,	April 29, 1818,	Deceased.			
191	Mary Henderson,	March 10, 1820,	Sept. 20, 1852,			Issue traced in the Barber connection.
†192	Adeline Henderson,	Dec. 4, 1821,	Deceased.			
193	James Henderson,	Jan. 15, 1826,	Deceased.			
194	Jane Elizabeth Henderson,	March 9, 1828,		March 2, 1859,	Thomas K. Barber,	
195	Ambrose Henderson,	March 16, 1831,			L. Rynearson.	
†196	Margaret Elmer Henderson,	July 19, 1833,	Dec. 13, 1868.		Cornelia Burrows.	
44	WILLIAM and MARGARET CLYDE BARBER.					
197	Elizabeth Ann Barber,	Nov. 2, 1820,			Amos T. Bisel,	Bloomsburg, Columbia Co., Pa.
198	Mary Barber,	Sept. 2, 1823,			Martin Girton,	Jerseytown, Columbia Co., Pa.
199	Sarah Savilla Barber,	July 2, 1826,			Hiram Masteller,	Jerseytown, Columbia Co., Pa.
†200	Nancy Jane Barber,	July 2, 1826,	March 18, 1831.			

No.	NAME.	BIRTH, Date and Place.	DEATH, Date and Place.	MARRIAGE, Date and Place.	TO WHOM MARRIED.	REMARKS.
†201	Wm. Findley Barber,	May 11, 1829,	July 26, 1829.		Matthias Appleman,	Jerseytown, Columbia Co., Pa.
202	Margaret Jane Barber,	Sept. 2, 1833,				
45	ROBERT and ELIZABETH BARBER MOORHEAD.					
†203	Thomas Moorhead,		Deceased,	Married,		Mansfield, O.
204	James Moorhead,					Mansfield, O.
205	Son.					
206	Clarissa Moorhead,			Married,		Mansfield, O.
46	DANIEL and SARAH MOORHEAD BARBER.					
†207	Martha W. Barber,	Feb. 20, 1822,	May 29, 1863,		Robert Blue,	Had 2 children, both died in infancy.
208	John M. Barber,	Oct. 7, 1825,	Dec., 1865,		Nancy McAfee,	Presbyterian.
209	Mary W. Barber,	July 23, 1827,			Wilson McAlister,	Presbyterian.
†210	Thos. M. Barber,	Jan. 7, 1830,	Nov. 24, 1854,		Unmarried.	
†211	Phineas M. Barber,	April 3, 1832,			Margaret Marr,	No issue. Repub.; Presb.; Merchant. Philadelphia.
†212	James Barber,	May 7, 1835,	Oct. 5, 1854,		Unmarried.	
†213	Maggie S. Barber,	April 17, 1837,	Sept. 24, 1857,		Unmarried.	
47	JOHN and SARAH BARBER McCOLLUM.					
†213½	Catharine McCollum,	1823,	1835.	Married.		
214	E. J. McCollum,	1825,		1853,	Margaret Marr.	
215	Ephraim J. McCollum,	1827,		1857,	James Moorhead.	
†216	Margaret McCollum,	1829,		1877,	William Flock.	
†217	Ellen McCollum,					
	2D HUSBAND, PETER WEIGLE.					
†218	Elizabeth Weigle,		Dead.	Married,		Richland. History not known.
219	Mary Weigle,			Married,		Richland. " "
220	William Weigle,			Married,		Richland. " "
221	Hannah Weigle,					

No.	NAME.	BIRTH, Date and Place.	DEATH, Date and Place.	MARRIAGE, Date and Place.	TO WHOM MARRIED.	REMARKS.
49	JESSE and MARY FUNSTON BARBER.					
222	Andrew Barber,	Jan. 17, 1821,	. . .	1850,	Lucy Ann Claypool.	
†223	Nicholas Funston Barber,	Dec. 25, 1825,	. . .		Unmarried.	
224	Franklin Barber,	Dec. 31, 1827,	. . .		Ann Brittain.	
225	John Barber,	Oct. 24, 1830,	. . .	June 10, 1856,	K. E. Follmer.	
226	Silas W. Barber,	1833.	. . .	Dec. 18, 1860,	John Fruit.	
227	Harriet Barber,	Oct. 5, 1836,	May 19, 186?	Feb. 1, 1866,		
†228	James Barber,	Jan. 15, 1839,	. . .	Dec. 15, 1864,	Nancy Dilden.	
229	William Barber,	April 10, 1841,	. . .			
52	JAMES and JANE CLYDE KENNEDY.					
230	James Clyde Kennedy,	. . .	. . .	. . .	Hetty K. Sherrard,	Doctor: Dem. Stewartsville, N. J.
53	JOHN and SARAH KENNEDY KERR.					
230¼	Margaret Kennedy Kerr,	. . .	Deceased.	. . .	Ira Sheldon.	
230½	Jane Eliza Kerr,	. . .	Deceased.	. . .		
231	Mary S. Kerr,	. . .	Deceased.	. . .		
†232	Thomas K. Kerr,	. . .	. . .	. . .	Cynthia Wallace.	
233	James Kerr,	. . .	. . .	. . .	Daniel Munger.	
234	Caroline Margaret Kerr,	. . .	. . .	. . .		
†235	Joseph Kerr,	. . .	Deceased.	. . .	John James Davis.	
236	Louisa Kerr,	. . .	. . .	. . .		
54	ALEXANDER and JANE KENNEDY INNES.					
237	Margaret Innes,	. . .	. . .	. . .	G. H. Cline,	Physician. Harmony, N. J.
238	Mary Innes,	. . .	. . .	. . .	William Carpenter.	
55	ADAM and MARGARET KENNEDY RUNKLE.					
†239	William Runkle.					
240	Margaret Runkle,	. . .	. . .	. . .	Edward F. Stewart,	{ Lawyer; Merchant. Easton, Pa. Presbyterian.

No.	NAME.	BIRTH, Date and Place.	DEATH, Date and Place.	MARRIAGE, Date and Place.	TO WHOM MARRIED.	REMARKS.
57	George W. and Elizabeth Kennedy Barber.					
241	Robert K. Barber,		Deceased.		Mary ——.	
†242	Thomas K. Barber,					
†243	Jessie Barber,					
†244	Isaac C. Barber.					
†245	Sarah Barber.					
†246	John Stewart Barber.				Hetty Martel.	
†247	James K. Barber,					
†248	Stewart Barber.					
†249	Charles D. Barber.					
58	Robert S. and Catherine Stuart Kennedy.					
†250	Thomas Kennedy,		Deceased.			No issue.
†251	Mary F. Kennedy,				James McWilliams,	Episcopal Preacher.
252	Margaret S. Kennedy,				Charles S. Kellogg,	
†253	Henry Martyn Kennedy.					
254	S. Louisa Kennedy,				Samuel D. Carpenter.	
255	James M. Kennedy,				Mary Carter.	
62	James J. and Margaret Cowell Kennedy.					
†256	William S. Kennedy,	Aug. 20, 1820.	Aug. 22.			
257	Ellen H. Kennedy,	Aug. 11, 1822.		May 14, 1844,	Edmund Culbertson,	Doctor; Presbyterian. Chambersburg. Republican.
258	Joseph C. Kennedy,	May 15, 1825,		April 6, 1862.	Catherine Smith,	Presbyterian; Farmer Democrat. Junction City, Kan.
⊛259	Thomas B. Kennedy,	Aug. 1, 1827,		April 22, 1856,	Ariana Stuart Riddle,	Attorney; Democrat; Presbyterian. Chambersburg.
260	Emmeline Kennedy.	June 11, 1829,		Oct. 5, 1847,	William L. Chambers,	Presbyterian; Lawyer: Republican. Chambersburg.
261	Maxwell Kennedy.	Nov. 16, 1831,			Martha Orr,	Doctor; Democrat; Presbyterian. Junction City, Kan.
262	James Kennedy,	Nov. 8, 1834,			Emma Grey,	Pres.; Dem.; Farmer. Junction City.
†263	Margaret Kennedy,	June 12, 1858,	Died in infancy.			
264	John Logan Kennedy,	Nov. 8, 1840,		Not married,		Ranching; Democrat. California.

No.	NAME.	BIRTH, Date and Place.	DEATH, Date and Place.	MARRIAGE, Date and Place.	TO WHOM MARRIED.	REMARKS.
63	**WILLIAM MAXWELL and MARIA KERR KENNEDY.**					
265	Jane Kennedy,				Unmarried.	
266	Sarah Kennedy,				Mr. Wyckoff.	
64	**STEWART and ANN FERGUSON KENNEDY.**					
267	Sarah Kennedy,	Feb. 11, 1822,	Aug. 25, 1855,	April 9, 1850,	J. Craig McLanahan,	Elder Presb. Church; Republican. Greencastle, Pa.
268	James Ferguson Kennedy,	Sept. 27, 1824,		July 6, 1852,	Louisa Weiss McKinley,	Presb. Preacher: Blind; Democrat. Chambersburg. A very highly esteemed gentleman.
269	Matilda Kennedy,	Oct. 1, 1827,		May 17, 1855,	Edward A. Lesley,	Attorney: Presbyterian. Philada.
†270	Elmira Kennedy,	March 30, 1830,	April 1, 1841,			
†271	Stewart Kennedy,	Sept. 13, 1833,	March 8, 1864,		Unmarried,	Surgeon U. S. N.; Democrat. Chambersburg.
272	William Kennedy,	Sept. 22, 1838,			{ 1 w. Ellen Culbertson,- 2 w. Mary Hauch, }	Editor: Democrat: Presbyterian. Chambersburg.
66	**PHINEAS BARNET and PRISCILLA CARR KENNEDY.**					
273	Sarah Jane Kennedy,				Henry Reeves,	Presb. Preacher. Gloucester, N. J.
274	William Kennedy,				Margaret Van Buskirk,	
275	Alfred Kennedy,				{ 1 w. Hattie Sharp, 2 w. Josephine Sharp, }	No issue. Missouri.
276	Francis Kennedy,		Died in infancy.			
277	Emma Kennedy,		Died in infancy.		Edwin F. Brewster.	
278	Edward Thomas Kennedy,		Died in infancy.			
279	Elizabeth Wilson Kennedy,					
280	Mary Bell Kennedy,		Died in infancy.			
281	John Carr Kennedy,		Died in infancy.		John F. Kennedy,	Traced in the other line—320.
282	P. B. Maxwell Kennedy,					
67	**GEORGE S. and SARAH KENNEDY GREEN.**					
283	William Henry Green.	Jan. 27, 1825,		{ June 24, 1852, April 28, 1855, }	{ 1 w. Elizabeth Caldwell. 2 w. Elizabeth Hayes. }	{ Presbyterian: Rev. D.D. LL.D. Princeton. Republican. }

No.	NAME.	BIRTH, Date and Place.	DEATH, Date and Place.	MARRIAGE, Date and Place.	To WHOM MARRIED.	REMARKS.
284	Sarah Elizabeth Green,	Nov. 8, 1828,	...	Dec. 30, 1852,	Rev. John Thomas Duffield, D.D.,	Presbyterian Preacher; Professor, Princeton.
285	Anna Corilla Green,	May 4, 1832,	...	Jan. 12, 1859, May 21, 1873,	1 h. Edward D. Yeomans. 2 h. Mireot S. Morgan.	
286	Edward T. Green,	June 8, 1837,	...	Oct. 20, 1860, June 20, 1865,	1 w. Julia Davenport Thompson. 2 w. Charlotte Higbee Beasley,	A prominent and influential Lawyer in Trenton, N. J. In addition to his position as attorney for the Pennsylvania R. R. Co., he has a large and lucrative private practice. Repub.; Presb.
68	MICHAEL and JANE MAXWELL KENNEDY CHRISTIAN.					
†287	James Kennedy Christian,	...	Died young.			
†288	Asa Dunan Christian,	...	Died young, ab't manhood.			
†289	Michael Clark Christian,	...				
290	Rebecca Elizabeth Christian	...			Almina Fisher.	
69	JAMES and MARY McWILLIAMS KENNEDY.				Joseph Medley.	
†291	Ann Kennedy,	...			Married. No issue.	California.
†292	Jos. McWilliams Kennedy,	...			Married twice. No issue.	
†293	Thomas Kennedy,	...	Died young.			
†294	William Kennedy,	...			Unmarried,	California.
†295	Samuel Kennedy,	...	Died young.			
†296	Mary Jane Kennedy,	...	Died young.			
†297	John Kennedy,	...	Died young.			
†298	Marion Stewart Kennedy,	...	Died young.			
70	THOMAS and SARAH SLOAN KENNEDY.					
298	William Sloan Kennedy,	...				Presbyterian Preacher. Died in Cincinnati, leaving a wife and four children.

No.	NAME.	BIRTH, Date and Place.	DEATH, Date and Place.	MARRIAGE, Date and Place.	TO WHOM MARRIED.	REMARKS.
299	Elizabeth Sarah Kennedy,				Mr. Willowby.	
300	Martha Kennedy,				Mr. East.	
†301	Margaret Kennedy,		Died young.			
302	Lydia Kennedy,					
303	Katherine Kennedy,					
304	Hannah Kennedy,					
305	Susan Kennedy,					
306	Zantha Kennedy,					
307	Emma Kennedy,		(Just entered maturity.)			
74	Robert and Margaret Johnston Kennedy.					
308	Charles Johnston Kennedy,				{ 1 w. Mary Welsh, . . / 2 w. Isabella McWilliams }	Democrat; Presbyterian.
†309	Andrew Jackson Kennedy,		Died young.			
†310	Elizabeth Kennedy,		Died young.		Married,	Two sons, both dead.
311	John Patterson Kennedy,		Died young.		Ellen Perling,	Lexington, Ill.
312	William H. Kennedy,		Died young.		Daniel Shaffer.	
313	Mary Jane Kennedy,					
311	Letitia Kennedy,				Unmarried,	St. Joseph Co., Ind.
†315	Alfred Brient Kennedy,				Madison Smith,	Niles, Mich.
316	James Stewart Kennedy,				Alsina Wells,	St. Joseph Co., Ind.
317	Emma F. Kennedy,					
318	Sarah Ann Kennedy,					
75	Robert Montgomery and Mary Buttles Kennedy.					
319	Samuel P. Kennedy,	Mar. 15, 1829.		April 26, 1852,	Frances A. Dray,	{ M.D. Served in the war as a surgeon. Marion, Linn Co., Iowa. Dem.
319½	Mary Jane Kennedy,	July 29, 1821,	June 2, 1874.	July 4, 1843,	Randall Simmons,	Baptist: Republican: Farmer. Howland, Ohio.
320	Adaline Kennedy,	Oct. 11, 1823,		{ June 21, 1848, / Jan. 31, 1858,	{ John Wise, . . . / P. H. McDerniel,	Minnesota. Christian: Farmer.
320½	Amanda B. Kennedy,	July 8, 1828,		Nov. 2, 1854,	Isaac Heaton,	Farmer, Trumbull Co., O. Dem.
321	Joel B. Kennedy,	July 25, 1831.		Mar. 19, 1851,	Margaret Boyes,	Trumbull Co. Ohio. Baptist.
†322	Temperance Ann Kennedy,	Feb. 21, 1834,	April 1, 1856,		{ Harrison Pearce, two children. All dead,	Howland. Dem.; Carriage maker.

No.	NAME.	BIRTH, Date and Place.	DEATH, Date and Place.	MARRIAGE, Date and Place.	TO WHOM MARRIED.	REMARKS.
323	Francis Marion Kennedy,	Jan. 7, 1837,		April 10, 1861,	Jerushia E. Post,	Minnesota. Dem.; Presb.; Farmer.
324	Elizabeth M. Kennedy,	Nov. 14, 1839,	Jan. 22, 1875,	July 12, 1857,	Albert Blanchard,	Minnesota. Republican. Spiritualist; County Clerk. No issue reported.
325	Austa C. Kennedy,			April 11, 1859,	Edward J. Boyes,	Minnesota. Farmer.
76	DAVID B. and JANE KENNEDY KING.					
326	Mary Jane King,	March 16, 1822,			Gustavus Wilson,	Warren, O.
327	S. S. King,				Abigail Chamberlain,	Farmer, Howland. Republican.
328	Samuel King,				Elizabeth Sutliff,	Mecca, O.
329	Caroline King,				Edward Felin,	Howland, O.
330	Amanda King,				James Phillips,	Howland, O.
77	SAMUEL and NANCY KENNEDY KING.					
331	Olive King,	Oct. 12, 1816,	Oct. 23, 1844,		James Wilson,	Farmer. Howland Co., O.
332	Samuel K. King,	May 2, 1818,	Jan. 27, 1853,			
333	Anna King,	April 15, 1820,			Unmarried,	Howland, O.
334	Jane K. King,	May 8, 1822,			Simon L. Abell,	Warren, O.
335	James B. King,	July 20, 1826,	Aug. 21, 1827,			Warren, O.
336	Thomas K. King,	Oct. 22, 1829,	Sept. 31, 1851,			Howland, O.
78	WILLIAM and MARY BARBER KENNEDY KING.					
337	James F. King,	March 12, 1822,		Sept. 16, 1862,	Cornelia Andrews,	(Whig; Republican. Extensive breeder of fine stock. Howland, O.
338	Irene King,	Jan. 24, 1824,	July 19, 1826,			
339	Anna Orilla King,	July 22, 1826,		Dec. 2, 1847,	William Chamberlain,	Trumbull Co., O. Farmer; Repub.
340	Jerushia King,	May 15, 1829,		May 9, 1850,	Charles R. Hunt,	(Episcopalian; Republican; Banker. Warren, O.
79	THOMAS and PHEBE CASTERLINE KENNEDY.					
341	Permelia Kennedy,	March 31, 1839,			William H. Miller,	(United Brethren; Preacher. Cortland, O. Republican.

No.	NAME.	BIRTH, Date and Place.	DEATH, Date and Place.	MARRIAGE, Date and Place.	TO WHOM MARRIED.	REMARKS.
342	Philander Kennedy,	March 19, 1841.	Dec. 13, 1874.	August 2, 1869.	Eliza A. Chidsey.	
343	Adelia Kennedy,	Sept. 12, 1845.		Feb. 27, 1870.	Phelps G. Freer.	
344	Irene Kennedy,	Nov. 18, 1849.			Unmarried.	
345	Lucy C. Kennedy.	June 27, 1852.		Nov. 18, 1871.	Aylmer B. McCleary,	Disciple.
80	WILLIAM B. and ELIZA DAVIS KENNEDY.					
346	Anthony Wayne Kennedy.	Feb. 17, 1841.		April 22, 1868.	Eunice Kellogg.	Supt. Pub. Schools, Trumbull Co., O.
347	Ann Iddings Kennedy.	May 8, 1843.		Nov. 22, 1866.	Kennedy Andrews.	Merchant. Howland, O.
348	Cassius Clay Kennedy.	Sept. 12, 1845.		Feb. 25, 1869.	Alice Kellogg.	Farmer: Teacher. Cortland, Ohio.
349	Judd D. Kennedy.	Dec. 23, 1848.	June 10, 1863.			
349½	Ella Kennedy.	May 24, 1851.	Nov. 12, 1851.			
81	JAMES and ALICE SCOTT KENNEDY.					
350	William Wallace Kennedy.	Dec. 12, 1832.		Sept. 18, 1862.	Sallie A. Sowers.	Farmer: Repub. Howland, Ohio.
351	George W. Kennedy.	May 16, 1836.		Nov. 11, 1865.	Eliza Bailey.	Farmer; Repub. Fought through the whole war; wounded several times. Howland, Ohio.
352	James L. Kennedy.	June 4, 1843.		Sept. 9, 1869.	Betsy Alderman.	Sec'y of Warren Waterworks; Repub.
353	John S. Kennedy.	August 20, 1850.		Nov. 29, 1876.	Jennie B. King.	Salesman; Republican.
82	MAXWELL and EVELIN DORD KENNEDY.					
354	Esther Ann Kennedy.	Jan. 7, 1836.		May 18, 1851.	Francis N. Andrews.	Howland, Ohio. Farmer; Repub.
355	Henry H. Kennedy.	Dec. 19, 1837.		Jan. 8, 1870.	Clara Harding.	Repub.: Fruit Farmer. Sierra, Cal.
356	Morris C. Kennedy.	Nov. 10, 1842.		Sept. 23, 1867.	Selind Reed.	Cortland, O. Repub.; Marble Yard.
357	Edwin Dord Kennedy.	Nov. 13, 1850.		Sept. 29, 1875.	Fannie M. Terry.	Lawyer; Repub. Warren, Ohio.
358	Helen M. Kennedy.	May 25, 1856.		Nov. 10, 1874.	M. B. Halstead.	Farmer; Repub. Howland, Ohio.
83	SAMUEL and TABITHA K. KENNEDY.					
		1822.	August, 1831.			
359	Ann Eliza Kennedy.	March 27, 1836.		Sept. 25, 1877.	Addie Ewing,	Warren. Farmer; Republican.
360	Wm. W. Kennedy.	August 14, 1841.				
361	Ann Eliza Kennedy.					

No.	NAME.	BIRTH. Date and Place.	DEATH. Date and Place.	MARRIAGE. Date and Place.	TO WHOM MARRIED.	REMARKS.
84	**MONTGOMERY and ELIZABETH KENNEDY ANDERSON.**					
†362	William Anderson,				Bethia McClurg.	No issue reported.
363	George Anderson,					
364	Harriet Anderson,				Mr. Cromwell.	
†365	Samuel Anderson,		Died young.			
86	**JACOB and JANE YOUNG BEAR.**					
†366	John Y. Bear,	Nov. 20, 1813.	Dec. 10, 1838.	August 1, 1836.	Horatio A. Stearns.	Doctor. Beaver Co., Pa.
†367	Elizabeth Bear,	Jan. 17, 1817.	Dec. 28, 1858.			Methodist Preacher. Madison, O.
368	Richard M. Bear,	August 18, 1818.			1 w. Mary McDowell. 2 w. Eliza J. Tait, 3 w.	Methodist Preacher. Jamestown, Pa. Formed the Erie Conference, 1841.
369	William M. Bear,	Nov. 1, 1820.		(Mar. 3, 1842. (June 26, 1849.	(1 w. Mary S. Sharp, (2 w. Mary S. Clark,	Methodist Preacher. Bigelow, Minn. Joined the Erie Conference, 1846. Transferred to Minnesota Conference in 1872.
370	Ellen A. Bear,	Sept. 22, 1822.	March 18, 1852.		Cyrus Clark,	Pres. of Railroad. New Castle, Pa.
371	Addie Y. Bear,	July 12, 1824.				Salem, Ohio.
372	Chas. Wesley Bear,	Oct. 23, 1826.	Oct. 26, 1865.		Ann Paneake.	Meth. Preacher. New Castle, Pa.
373	Robert H. Bear,	Feb. 28, 1828.	June 31, 1848.			Farmer. Beaver Co., Pa
†374	Martha J. Bear,	March 23, 1830.	Jan. 15, 1849.			
375	Mary F. Bear,	April 1, 1832.			James Woodruff,	Iron Moulder. Salem, Ohio.
376	James Kennedy Bear,	Jan. 29, 1835.			Maria Gaily,	Farmer. Mt. Jackson, Pa. Served in Battery B, 1st Pa. Cavalry.
88	**WILLIAM and MARIA YOUNG COWHICK.**					
377	Anna Elizabeth Cowhick.	Jan. 4, 1818.			1 h. Pierson Bates, 2 h. Thos. Jefferson Phillis. 3 h. Samuel New.	Machinist. Carroll Co., Ohio.
†378	Ellen Cowhick,	1819.	Died in infancy. 1856.		Unmarried.	Farmer. Beaver Co., Pa.
†379	Joseph Benson Cowhick,	1823.			Unmarried.	Farmer. Bryan, Ohio.
380	John Young Cowhick,	Oct. 17, 1824.				Printer. Canton, Ohio.
†381	Maria Cowhick.	1826.	Died in infancy.			Self-educated Presb. Preacher. Cheyenne, W. T.

No.	NAME.	BIRTH. Date and Place.	DEATH. Date and Place.	MARRIAGE, Date and Place.	TO WHOM MARRIED.	REMARKS.
89	JAMES KENNEDY and JANE LOGAN MOORHEAD.					
382	MaxwellKennedy Moorhead	Sept. 5, 1831.	Jan. 29, 1855.	April 21, 1855.	Mary Heberton,	Manufacturer; Presb.; Republican. Pittsburgh.
†383	John Logan Moorhead,	Feb. 1, 1833,				
†384	Caroline Louisa Moorhead,	July 26, 1834,	Sept. 4, 1834.			
385	Mary Elizabeth Moorhead,	July 19, 1836,			Unmarried.	
386	Henrietta Louisa Moorhead,	August 7, 1838,			Unmarried.	Presb.; Repub. Pittsburgh. Capt. U. S. A.
387	Wm. Jefferson Moorhead,	Feb. 17, 1840,		Jan. 5, 1864.	Emily B. Black,	
†388	James Henry Moorhead,	Jan. 26, 1842.	Feb. 7, 1849.			
389	Jane Adeline Moorhead,	August 18, 1844.		Oct. 24, 1867.	James L. Murdock,	Doctor. Pittsburgh. Presb.; Repub.
90	JOS. BARLOW and ELIZABETH HILROSS MOORHEAD.					
390	Charles Hirons Moorhead,	Jan. 30, 1840.		Jan. 14, 1861.	Iney Phelps Hickman.	Iron Manuf.; Epis.; Repub. Phila.
391	Ada Elizabeth Moorhead,	Dec. 10, 1843.		Nov. 26, 1867.	George Clifford Thomas.	Epis.; Banker; Repub. Philadelphia.
392	Clara Alice Moorhead,	March 13, 1846.		April 22, 1868,	Jay Cooke, Jr.,	Epis.; Banker; Repub. Philadelphia.
393	Caroline Frances Moorhead,	March 13, 1846.		April 16, 1873.	Joseph Earlston Thropp.	Iron Master. Montgomery Co., Pa. Epis.; Republican.
91	WILLIAM G. and SARAH COOKE MOORHEAD.					
†394	Catherine Eliza Moorhead,	June 18, 1836,	May 4, 1852.		Unmarried,	Washington, D. C.
395	Wm. Elewtherns Moorhead,	July 26, 1839.				Washington, D. C. Banker.
396	Ysidora Beatrice Moorhead,	July 10, 1847,		April 30, 1874,	Henry Henly Dodge,	
95	WILLIAM and ELIZA MOORHEAD MONTGOMERY.					
†397	Charles M. Montgomery,		Died in infancy.			
†398	William M. Montgomery,		Died in infancy.			
399	Emily R. Montgomery,				S. L. Russel, (1 w. Rachel Anthony, 2 w. Mary Phelps,	Lawyer, Bedford, Pa. Presb.; Repub.; Printer; R. R. Contractor; Repub.; Presb. Missouri, Oregon.
100	James B. Montgomery,				Unmarried.	
401	Julia E. Montgomery,				Dr. T. S. Minor,	Port Townsend, Washington Ter.
402	Sarah E. Montgomery,					

No.	NAME.	BIRTH, Date and Place.	DEATH, Date and Place.	MARRIAGE, Date and Place.	TO WHOM MARRIED.	REMARKS.
†403	William H. Montgomery,	. . . .	Died in infancy.	. . . .	. . . .	
404	Ada J. Montgomery,	. . . .	. . . .	. . . .	James McCrea,	Engineer, Philadelphia. Republican. A man of distinction.
97	WILLIAM S. and MARGARET BYERS KENNEDY.					
405	James Bayers Kennedy,	Sept. 8, 1839,	. . . .	. . . .	Unmarried,	A talented Presb. Preacher Trenton.
†406	Howard C. Kennedy,	April 2, 1841,	May 4, 1842,	. . . .	. . . .	
†407	Theodore Tinlow Kennedy,	Dec. 18, 1842,	August 16, 1844.	. . . .	. . . .	
408	William Patton Kennedy,	Nov. 13, 1844.	. . . .	Oct. 10, 1878,	Not married,	Railroad Builder; Presb.; Repub. Lumber Merchant. Trenton. N. J.
409	Robert Wallace Kennedy,	Nov. 5, 1846.	. . . .	April 27, 1875,	Elizabeth B. Brearly.	Presbyterian; Republican.
410	Mary Letitia Kennedy,	Dec. 2, 1848.	. . . .	Nov. 9, 1876,	Rev. Samuel E. Webster.	Presbyterian Preacher.
411	Henry Martyn Kennedy,	Feb. 3, 1851.	. . . .	. . . .	Mary E. Jacobs,	Merchant: Repn. Mifflintown, Penna.
†412	Charles Green Kennedy,	Oct. 16, 1853.	Jan. 23, 1858.	. . . .	. . . .	
98	GEORGE and ANNA MARIA KENNEDY GREEN.					
413	Emma Kennedy Green,	Nov. 7, 1845,	. . . .	Dec. 8, 1869.	Fred. C. Lewis,	Merchant. Brooklyn, N.Y. Presb.
†413	Mary L. Green,	April 10, 1848.	March 31, 1850.	. . . .	. . . .	
99	JOHN H. and HARRIET McCALMONT KENNEDY.					
414	Ann Kittera Kennedy,	Nov. 16, 1828.	. . . .		Unmarried,	Presbyterian.
415	Robert Peebles Kennedy,	Feb. 3, 1831.	. . . .		Unmarried,	Presbyterian Preacher. Delaware.
†416	Geo. McCalmont Kennedy,	June 6, 1833.	1856.		Unmarried,	Engineer.
†417	James Maxwell Kennedy,	Jan. 5, 1856.	Sept. 20, 1871.		Unmarried,	Lawyer. California. Repub. Mason.
†418	Francis Herron Kennedy,	Feb. 5, 1839.	June 20, 1871.		Married. No issue.	Lawyer. California. Repub. Mason.
101	DAVID and NANCY DAVIDSON HURST.					
419	Robert Thomas Hunt,	August 30, 1835.	. . . .	. . . .	Unmarried,	Graduate Jefferson College; Studied Law with Judge Shaler; Soon abandoned the practice of Law for a Mercantile Life. Mason: Democrat. Pittsburgh.

No.	NAME.	BIRTH. Date and Place.	DEATH. Date and Place.	MARRIAGE. Date and Place.	TO WHOM MARRIED.	REMARKS.
120	John Davidson Hunt,	July 7, 1837,			Unmarried,	(Graduate Jefferson College; Clerk; Mason. Pittsburg. Republican.
†421	Luther Martin Hunt,	March 4, 1841,	Died in infancy.			
103	**JAMES MAXWELL and SI-BILLA S. MORRIS KENNEDY.**					
422	Herbert Morris Kennedy,	Sept. 25, 1837,			Arabella Buck,	(Methodist; Democrat; Farmer; McLean Co., Ill. Episcopalian.
423	Amelia Theresa Kennedy,	March 3, 1840,			Unmarried.	
†424	James Maxwell Kennedy,		Died in infancy.			
105	**LEWIS and MARY ANN KENNEDY MARTIN.**					
†425	Robert Kennedy Martin,	May 31, 1841,	Dec. 17, 1867.	Nov. 20, 1867.	Jennie B. Simpson,	(Served through the war with credit. Delphi, Ind.
426	Mary Elizabeth Martin,	Oct. 18, 1843,		Nov. 10, 1864.	Edward W. Barnes,	Presb.; Merchant. Delphi, Ind.
427	Emma Bell Martin,	April 14, 1845,	Feb. 22, 1851.	Jan. 20, 1869.	A. P. Cory,	McLean Co., Ill.
†428	William Thomas Martin,	Feb. 10, 1851,				
†429	Sibilla Jane Kennedy Martin,	Jan. 6, 1849,	Sept. 2, 1850.			
†430	Edward Martin,	Oct. 30, 1853,	May 7, 1872.			
†431	Henry Lewis Martin,	Feb. 16, 1847,	Oct. 5, 1848.			
432	Ella Martin,	June 26, 1857.		Sept. 26, 1878.	Horace McClure.	Danvers, Ill. Farmer.
107	**ELIAS DAVIDSON and AGNES SHIELDS CLARKE KENNEDY.**					
433	Alice Kennedy,	Dec. 27, 1856,		Oct. 21, 1876.	Robert Henry Clay Hill,	Merchant; Repub.; Presb. Phila.
434	Davidson Kennedy,	April 22, 1859,				Repub.; Broker. Phila. Presb.
†435	Clarke Kennedy,	Jan. 21, 1862,	August 7, 1861.			
436	Charles Clarke Kennedy,	July 21, 1861,				
437	Eliza Clarke Kennedy,	Oct. 3, 1866,				
438	Albert Edward Kennedy,	May 9, 1869,				
†439	Howard Kennedy,	March 19, 1872,	Dec. 1, 1874.			

No.	NAME.	BIRTH, Date and Place.	DEATH, Date and Place.	MARRIAGE, Date and Place.	TO WHOM MARRIED.	REMARKS.
113	JAMES and ANNA D. FINNEY LOGAN.					
440	John Finney Logan,				Virginia Knight.	
441	Emma Logan,				Unmarried.	
114	JOHN T. and Mrs. HENRIETTA BRYAN KENNEDY LOGAN.					
442	Mary Logan,	Feb. 18, 1841.			Unmarried.	Merchant; Presb. Pittsburgh.
443	George Bryan Logan,	Dec. 21, 1845.		Feb. 22, 1870.	Fanny Grant Lyon,	
444	Edward Payson Logan,	Jan. 5, 1847.		Sept. 1870.	Annie Clark.	
445	John Howard Logan,	Dec. 11, 1848.			Unmarried.	
446	Thomas Dale Logan,	Jan. 26, 1850.		Mar. 22, 1877.	Carrie B. Maloney.	
447	Henrietta Bryan Logan,	Jan. 29, 1852.		Jan. 1876.	Charles Hodge Scott.	
115	WILLIAM H. and MARY K. LOGAN BOYD.					
448	Elizabeth L. Boyd,	Jan. 1, 1828.	April 3, 1830.	Jan. 16, 1845.	Charles T. Stewart.	Washington, D. C.
†449	Sarah Boyd,	Jan. 6, 1829.		Dec. 26, 1861.	Agnes M. Copeland.	Pittsburgh.
450	John Logan Boyd,	June 6, 1831.		Oct. 16, 1865.	Harriet Cline.	Washington, N. J.
451	Henry Boyd,	Aug. 16, 1834.		Oct. 9, 1855.	Adam W. Bowman.	Washington, N. J.
452	Mary Jane Boyd,	Feb. 22, 1836.		Feb. 25, 1867.	Sarah H. James.	Burlington, N. J.
453	William H. Boyd,	Oct. 9, 1838.		Aug. 12, 1863.	Samuel E. Craft.	Washington, N. J.
454	Nancy C. Boyd,	May 6, 1841.		Jan. 1, 1869.	Lydia A. Wandling.	Washington, N. J.
455	James L. Boyd,	Sept. 7, 1843.				Dayton, W. T.
456	Thomas McKeen Boyd,	May 19, 1850.				
†457	Edward Green Boyd,	Oct. 16, 1855.	Feb. 11, 1852.	May 24, 1877.	William G. Creveling.	Washington, N. J.
458	Henrietta Logan Boyd,					
117	ROBERT T. and CHARLOTTE HAMBRIGHT KENNEDY.					
459	Margareta Kennedy,	Jan. 19, 1835.		Nov. 20, 1851. 1869.	{ 1 h. W. C. Carr. { 2 h. S. D. Kane.	Episcopalian. Memphis, Tenn. Catholic. Memphis, Tenn.
460	Lillie E. Kennedy,	Nov. 25, 1836.		Dec. 31, 1857.	George Shiras.	A distinguished Lawyer. Pittsburgh. Republican.
461	Emma L. Kennedy,	Aug. 14, 1838.		Jan. 18, 1866.	William H. Forsyth,	Merchant; Presb.; Repub. Pittsburgh.

No.	NAME.	BIRTH, Date and Place.	DEATH, Date and Place.	MARRIAGE, Date and Place.	TO WHOM MARRIED.	REMARKS.
462	Fred. H. Kennedy,	April 23, 1840,		May 28, 1868,	Kate Brown,	R. R. Clerk: Presb.: Repub., Pittsburgh.
463	Alice Mary Kennedy,	April 10, 1843,		June 22, 1865,	William R. Howe,	Manufacturer: Epis.: Republican. Pittsburgh.
464	William M. Kennedy,	Dec. 29, 1844,		Feb. 17, 1875,	Eliza McClintock,	Flour Mills: Repub., Pittsburgh.
465	Bessie E. Kennedy,	June 30, 1846,		Jan. 12, 1876,	C. H. Call,	Powder Mills, Michigan.
466	Sara S. Kennedy,	March 28, 1848,		June 14, 1871,	F. B. Speer,	Merchant, Michigan.
†467	Robert T. Kennedy,	Jan. 17, 1851,	April, 1856,			
†468	Adelaide H. Kennedy,	Aug. 11, 1855,	August 8, 1855.			
469	Jeanie Maxwell Kennedy,			Dec. 1, 1879,	J. G. Reynolds,	Powder Mills. Michigan.
118	**Winfield Scott and Mauvina Slaymaker Kennedy.**					
†470	William Maxwell Kennedy,		Deceased.		Unmarried.	
471	John Matthias Kennedy,				Florence Graddy.	
119	**Sylvester and Martha A. Kinzer Kennedy.**					
472	Henry Kinzer Kennedy,		Deceased.		Smith Paterson Buyers,	Lancaster Co., Pa.
473	Margaret Maxwell Kennedy,					Lancaster Co., Pa.
474	Maxwell Kennedy,					Lancaster Co., Pa.
475	Philip Timlow Kennedy,					Lancaster Co., Pa.
476	George Clemens Kennedy,			Dec. 19, 1876,		Lancaster, Pa. Lawyer.
477	Alonzo Potter Kennedy,					Lancaster Co., Pa.
478	Horace Elliott Kennedy,					Lancaster Co., Pa.
120	**William M. and Henrietta B. Kennedy.**					
479	Anna Margaret Kennedy,	Aug. 11, 1835,	May 11, 1875,	Oct. 1863,	David C. Marquis,	Presbyterian Preacher. Baltimore.
121	**Andrew and Jane E. Kennedy Buyers.**					
480	Josephine Y. Buyers,				R. S. McIlvaine,	Lancaster Co., Pa.
481	Maxwell K. Buyers,					Lancaster Co., Pa.
482	Letitia A. Buyers,				W. D. Rounds,	Lancaster Co., Pa.

No.	NAME.	BIRTH, Date and Place.	DEATH, Date and Place.	MARRIAGE, Date and Place.	TO WHOM MARRIED.	REMARKS.
483	Patton L. Buyers,					Lancaster Co., Pa.
484	Margaretta K. Buyers,				Edwin Ewing,	Lancaster Co., Pa.
127	Robert Kennedy and Maria Heasric Reading.					
485	Eliza Reading,				Edward Remington,	Philadelphia.
486	Mary Reading,				John P. Grandon.	
487	Frank Reading,				Miss Hepburn.	
488	Elmina Reading,				Alex. Gitlick.	
†489	Sims H. Reading,				Unmarried.	
490	Charlton Reading,				Miss Sprole.	
491	Harrison Reading,				Married a widow,	One son.
128	De Pey and his wife Theodoria Reading.					
492	John Robert K. De Pey.					
128	Gen. Isaac G. and Theodoria Reading De Pey Farley.					
493	Reading Farley,				Miss Scudder.	
494	Anna Farley,				Hon. A. G. Richey.	
495	George Farley,				Miss Opdyke.	
†496	Eliza Farley,				Peter Cox. No issue.	
132	John and Elizabeth Kennedy Reading Grandon.					
†497	Daniel Reading Grandon,				Unmarried.	
498	Mary Grandon,				Mr. Sloakum.	
†499	John Grandon,			1880.	Mrs. Todd.	
500	Jane Grandon,				Unmarried.	

No.	NAME.	BIRTH, Date and Place.	DEATH, Date and Place.	MARRIAGE, Date and Place.	TO WHOM MARRIED.	REMARKS.
133	WILLIAM and EUPHEMIA READING KENNEDY.					
501	Reading Kennedy,	...	...		...	Lawyer. Jersey City.
134	SYLVESTER and HANNAH COOK MATLACK SCOVEL.					
502	Mary Scovel,	...	...		F. L. Senour,	Presb. Preacher. Pittsburgh. Repub.
503	James M. Scovel,	...	...		Mary Mulford.	Distinguished Lawyer. President of State Senate: Presbyterian: Republican. Camden, N. J.
504	Sallie Scovel,	...	...		Edward Shields.	Presb. Preacher. Cape May. N. J.
*505	Sylvester F. Scovel,	...	...		Caroline Woodruff.	Distinguished Doctor of Divinity in the Presbyterian Church: Republican. Pittsburgh, Pa.
506	Harriet Scovel,	...	...		Charles Alling.	Madison, Ind. Merchant.
507	Hannah Scovel,	...	...		Richard Muzzy,	Springfield, O. Merchant: Presb.: Republican.
508	Kitty Scovel.	...	...		Mr. Burrowes,-	Franklin, O. Brewer,
509	Belle Scovel,	...	...		J. D. Barnett.	St. Mary's Parish, La. Planter: Presbyterian: Democrat.
510	Robert A. Scovel,	...	...		Clara Cobb..	Chicago. Presbyterian: Republican.
135	ROBERT KENNEDY and AUBEY LEAMING MATLOCK.					
511	Lizzie Matlock,	...	...			Woodbury, N. J.
512	Mary Matlock,	...	...			Woodbury, N. J.
513	Ellen Matlock,	...	...			Woodbury, N. J.
514	Charlotte Matlock,	...	...			Woodbury, N. J.
515	Leaming Matlock,	...	...			Woodbury, N. J.
516	Robert Kennedy Matlock, Jr.,	...	...			Woodbury, N. J.
136	ABRAM and ELIZABETH KENNEDY BROWNING.					
†516	Robert Matlock Browning,	...	Deceased,	Unmarried,		Lawyer: Epis.: Dem. Camden, N.J.

No.	NAME.	BIRTH, Date and Place.	DEATH, Date and Place.	MARRIAGE, Date and Place.	TO WHOM MARRIED.	REMARKS.
517	Gertrude Browning.	. . .	. . .	Miss White.		
518	George G. Browning.	. . .	. . .			
519	Beulah Browning.	. . .	. . .			
137	Jeanne Robert and Eliz-abeth La Grange Fre-linghuysen Kennedy.					
520	John Frelinghuysen Kennedy,	Feb. 7, 1840.	. . .	. . .	Mary B. Kennedy, daughter of Phin. B. Kennedy.	See 280.
†521	Miriam Kay Kennedy,	Sept. 30, 1841.	. . .	. . .		
522	Robt. Henric Kennedy, Jr.,	May 12, 1843.	Nov. 7, 1861.			
523	Theodore Frelinghuysen Kennedy,	May 9, 1846.	. . .	Sept. 18, 1864. / Sept. 7, 1874.	1 w. Arabella Williamson. / 2 w. Rachel Warne.	
524	Beulah Elizabeth Kennedy,	Dec. 22, 1848.	. . .	Nov. 21, 1871.	Mary Carpenter, daughter of Wm. Carpenter,	See 652. Farmer, N. J.
†525	Louisa Frelinghuysen Kennedy,	Nov. 25, 1856.	May 18, 1873.		Theodore B. Hanee.	
163	Joseph Marr and First Wife.					
526	Catherine Marr.	. . .	Deceased,	. . .	David McCormick.	Harrisburg, Pa.
527	John Marr,	. . .	Deceased,	. . .		Left children.
528	Joseph Marr,	. . .	Deceased,	. . .		Left two children.
529	William Marr.	. . .	Died young.	Married.		Left children.
530	Second Wife.					
531	Harriet Marr.	. . .			General J. Irwin Gregg,	A distinguished Cavalry Officer; Presb.; Repub. Lewisburg, Pa.
	Third Wife.					
532	James Marr.	. . .			Kate Knight, Germantown.	A brave and gallant Officer during the entire war.
533	M. Elizabeth Marr.	. . .			Frank Killeman.	A gentleman of culture and taste: Musician; Ranch; Catholic; a large family.

No.	NAME.	BIRTH, Date and Place.	DEATH, Date and Place.	MARRIAGE, Date and Place.	TO WHOM MARRIED.	REMARKS.
534	J. Josephine Marr	. . .	. . .	. . .	{ 1 h. Donovan, 2 h. Gustave A. Breaux, }	Both husbands Lawyers, Catholics, and Democrats. Both members of the Legislature in their respective states. Breaux was a Colonel in the Rebel Army.
535	Angeline Marr,	. . .		. . .	Henry Knight, . . .	Germantown, Pa. Merchant: Republican; Presbyterian.
†536			Died in infancy.			
164	PHINEAS B. and MARY GRAHAM MARR.					
†537	Mary Jane Marr,	. . .		. . .	Dr. J. E. Barber,	No issue.
†538	William Marr,	. . .		. . .	Not married.	
†539	Henry Marr,	. . .		. . .	Caroline Gold, . .	No issue.
†540	James Marr,	. . .		. . .	Not married.	Presbyterian Preacher.
541	Adison Marr,	. . .		. . .	Margaret Sheriff.	
†542	Margaret Marr,	. . .		. . .	P. M. Barber,	Merchant; Presb.; Repmb. Philada.
543	Helen Marr,	. . .		. . .	J. W. Crawford.	
†544	Augustus Marr,	. . .		Deceased.	Unmarried. . .	Preacher. Princeton, N. J.
†545	Caddie Marr,	. . .				
†546	Henrietta Marr,	. . .		Deceased.		
†547	Walter Marr,	. . .			Not married.	
165	PHINEAS BARBER and his wife SUSANNA MARR.					
†548	Hannah Barber,	. . .		. . .	. . .	Fingal, Canada.
549	William Barber,	. . .		. . .	. . .	Fingal, Canada.
550	John Barber,	. . .		. . .	. . .	Fingal, Canada.
551	James Barber,	. . .		. . .	. . .	Fingal, Canada.
†552	David Barber,	. . .		. . .	. . .	Fingal, Canada.
†553	Daniel Barber,	. . .		. . .	. . .	Fingal, Canada.
166	ANN MARR and SAMUEL BOWMAN.					
554	Joseph Bowman,	. . .		. . .	Dr. Gun.	
555	Albert Bowman,	. . .		. . .	Married.	

No.	NAME.	BIRTH, Date and Place.	DEATH, Date and Place.	MARRIAGE, Date and Place.	TO WHOM MARRIED.	REMARKS.
556	James Bowman.					
557	Jonas Bowman.					
558	Henrietta Bowman,					
559	Charles Bowman.					
163	**David Price Marr.** 1 w. Hatty L. Davis. 2 w. Harriet Marcus.			Feb. 13, 1878,	N. A. Hughs.	
560	Anna Eliza Marr.	Oct. 30, 1840,		Sept. 24, 1861,	John A. Grier.	Chester Co., Pa. Fleet Chief Engineer during the war; now in the Mint, at Philadelphia.
†561	William Marr,	Nov. 20, 1842,	Aug. 30, 1850.	June, 1861.	John McCleery.	Milton, Pa. No issue reported.
†562	Mary Helen Marr,	Nov. 9, 1844,				
†563	Rebecca L. Marr,	Feb. 11, 1847,	April 4, 1850.			
†564	David Brainerd Marr,	Nov. 6, 1856,			Unmarried.	
†565	Alfred Marr,				Unmarried.	
†566	Janette Dales Marr,				Unmarried.	
†567	William Price Marr,	Dec. 21, 1851,	Jan. 1870.			Killed whilst crossing a railroad track.
568	Alem Kennedy Marr.	Dec. 25, 1854.			Ellie Schofield.	New York; now Prince George, Md.
170	**William H. and Eliza Davis Baldwin Marr.**					
†568½			Died in infancy.			
†568¾			Died in infancy.			
†568⅞			Died in infancy.			
†569			Died in infancy.			
570	James Marr,				Married.	Sunbury, Pa.
571	Frank Marr.				Not married.	Lawyer. Sunbury, Pa.
172	**Phineas and Susan Mann Barber.**					
572	William Barber,					Fingal, Canada.
572¼	Hannah Barber,					Fingal, Canada.
572½	John Barber,					Fingal, Canada.
572¾	James Barber,					Fingal, Canada.
573	David Barber,					Fingal, Canada.
573½	Daniel Barber,					Fingal, Canada.

No.	NAME.	BIRTH. Date and Place.	DEATH. Date and Place.	MARRIAGE. Date and Place.	TO WHOM MARRIED.	REMARKS.
173	**LESLIE** and **JANE BARBER PIERCE.**					
572	John Pierce.					
573	Hannah Pierce.					
574	Francis Pierce.					
571	Mary Pierce.					
574	Martha Pierce.					
575	Annie Pierce.					
575	Leslie Pierce.					
175	**DONALDSON** and **SARAH ISCENT BARBER.**					Fingal, Canada.
575½	Fannie Barber, ...					
179	**JAMES McCURLEY.**					
575½	—— McCurley.					
194	**JANE ELIZABETH HENDERSON** and her husband, L. **RYNERSON.**					
576	Son.					
577	Son.					
578	Son.					
195	**AMBROSE** and **CORNELIA BURROWS HENDERSON.**					
579	Elizabeth Henderson, . .	Feb. 22, 1860.				
580	Samuel Henderson, . .	April 27, 1862.				
581	Mary Henderson, . . .	Nov. 5, 1864.				
582	Gertrude Henderson, . .	March 11, 1867.				
583	Blanche Henderson, . .	Sept. 28, 1869.				
584	Charles Henderson, . .	Sept. 28, 1873.				
585	Adeline Henderson, . .	June 26, 1879.				

No.	NAME.	BIRTH, Date and Place.	DEATH, Date and Place.	MARRIAGE, Date and Place.	TO WHOM MARRIED.	REMARKS.
197	Amos T. and Elizabeth Ann Barber Bisel.					
586	Margaret Alice Bisel.				Jno. Jacob Everett.	Philadelphia.
587	Judith Emma Bisel.				Robt. Vanorman Leevers.	One child, deceased.
588	William Felix Bisel.				Annie Horn Coryell.	Lawyer, Philadelphia.
589	Daniel Levi Bisel.				Mary Strayer.	Philadelphia.
590	George Titus Bisel.					Philadelphia.
591	Susan Clyde Bisel.				Henry Clay Hartman.	Philadelphia.
198	Martin and Mary Barber Girton.					
592	Addison Girton.					
593	Maggie Girton.					
594						
595						
199	Hiram and Sarah Savilla Barber Masteller.					
596	Thaddeus Masteller.					
597	Susan Masteller.					
202	Matthias and Margaret Jane Barber Appleman.					
598	Mary Esther Appleman.					Rohrsburg, Columbia Co., Pa.
599	William Appleman.					Rohrsburg.
600	Philip Appleman.					Rohrsburg.
601	Clyde Appleman.					Rohrsburg.
602	George Appleman.					Rohrsburg.
603	Phineas Appleman.					Rohrsburg.
604	Name not given.					Rohrsburg.
208	John M. and Nancy McApee Barber.					
605	Daniel Barber.				Unmarried.	

No.	NAME.	BIRTH, Date and Place.	DEATH, Date and Place.	MARRIAGE, Date and Place.	TO WHOM MARRIED.	REMARKS.
209	WILSON and MARY W. BARBER McALISTER.					
†606	Oscar McAlister,	. . . .	Died in infancy.			
†607	Ellen McAlister,	. . . .	Deceased.	. . . .	S. B. Rank.	Clerk.
†608	Alice McAlister,	. . . .	Deceased.	. . . .	Unmarried, ...	
†609	Thomas McAlister,	. . . .	Deceased.			
†610	Jessie McAlister,	. . . .				
214	E. J. McCOLLUM.					
†611	Gaylord McCollum,	. . . .	Deceased.	. . . .	A. Cochran, ...	No issue.
†612	Leon McCollum,	. . . .	. . . .			
222	ANDREW and LACY ANN CLAYPOOL BARBER.					
613	Benjamin Franklin Barber,	Aug. 27, 1851,	. . . .	Dec. 15, 1874,	Jane Padgette.	
224	FRANKLIN and ANN BRITTAIN BARBER.					
†614	Alice Mary Barber,	April 17, 1857.				
†615	Benton Barber,	Feb. 15, 1859.				
616	Silas Barber,	Sept. 29, 1860.				
617	George F. Barber,	Oct. 18, 1861.	Jan. 5, 1861.			
618	Charles A. Barber,	Dec. 30, 1867.	Feb. 7, 1870.			
225	JOHN and K. E. FOLLMER BARBER.					
619	Daniel N. Barber,	Feb. 6, 1862.				
620	William Barber,	Sept. 13, 1866.				
227	JOHN and HARRIET BARBER FRUIT.					
621	Mary Robella Fruit,	Sept. 4, 1868.				

No.	NAME.	BIRTH, Date and Place.	DEATH, Date and Place.	MARRIAGE, Date and Place.	TO WHOM MARRIED.	REMARKS.
229	WILLIAM and NANCY DILLEN BARBER.					
†622	Myrtie Barber, . . .	Oct. 7, 1867,	July 4, 1875.			
†623	Hattie Barber, . . .	Feb. 22, 1870,	July 16, 1875.			
624	Nellie Barber, . . .	July 2, 1879				
230	JAMES CLYDE and HETTY K. SHERRARD KENNEDY.					
625	Jane C. Kennedy,				Dr. Samuel Clark.	Presbyterian. Belvidere, N. J.
626	Sarah Ann Kennedy, . .		1880,		Charles Corse,	(Elder Presb. Church: Lawyer. Lock Haven, Pa.
627	Samuel S. Kennedy, . .				Mary Stevens, . . .	Physician. Stewartsville, N. J.
231	IRA and MARY S. KERR SHELDEN.					
†628	Helen V. Shelden, . . .		Deceased,			Michigan.
†629	Sarah A. Shelden, . . .		Deceased,			Michigan.
233	JAMES and CYNTHIA WALLACE KERR.					
630	Kennedy Wallace Kerr, .				Married,	Michigan.
631	Mary C. Kerr, . . .					Michigan.
632	Sarah Kerr, . . .					Michigan.
234	DANIEL and CAROLINE M. KERR MUNGER.					
†633	John Kennedy Munger, .		Deceased,			Michigan.
†634	Thomas Kennedy Munger,		Deceased,			Michigan.
635	Lewis Edward Munger, .				Married,	Michigan.
636	Louisa Emma Munger, .					Michigan.
†637	Carrie Munger, . . .		Deceased,			Michigan.
638	Jessie Munger, . . .					Michigan.

No.	NAME.	BIRTH, DATE AND PLACE.	DEATH, DATE AND PLACE.	MARRIAGE, DATE AND PLACE.	TO WHOM MARRIED.	REMARKS.
236	JOHN JAMES and LOUISA KERR DAVIS.					
638	Herbert Jacob Davis, . .				Charlotte Rhodes.	Michigan.
237	GEORGE H. and MARGARET INNES CLINE.					
639	James T. Cline.				Emma Shipman.	Merchant. Centreville, Pa.
640	G. H. Cline, Jr., . .				Emma Stevenson.	Farmer. New Jersey.
641	Annie Cline,				Alonzo Miller, . .	Farmer. Harmony, N. J.
642	Horatio Cline, . .					Farmer. Harmony, N. J.
643	Frank P. Cline, . .					Bank Teller. Bloomsbury, N. J.
644	Charles H. Cline, . .					Doctor. Hainesburg, N. J.
645	Ernest L. Cline, . .					Harmony, N. J.
645½	Jane Cline, . .					Harmony, N. J.
645½	Mary Cline, . .					Harmony, N. J.
646	Elvira Cline, . .					Harmony, N. J.
647	Maggie Cline, . .					Harmony, N. J.
238	WILLIAM and MARY INNES CARPENTER.					
648	Joseph Carpenter, . .				Urana Riegel, . .	Prospector.
649	Margaret Carpenter, .				George De Witt, . .	Farmer.
650	Robert Carpenter, . .					Farmer.
651	James Carpenter, . .				Married, . . (Thomas Frelinghuysen Kennedy,	Farmer.
652	Mary Carpenter, . .			Nov. 21, 1871,		Traced in 532.
240	EDWARD F. and MARGARET RUNKLE STEWART.					
653	Laura Stewart, . .				Henry D. Lachenaur, .	Physician. Easton, Pa.
654	Ellen Moffatt Stewart, . .				Henry H. Baum, . .	Epis. Preacher. Easton, Pa.
241	ROBERT K. and MARY BARBER.					
655	Isaac Barber.					
656	George Barber.					
657	William Barber.					

39

No.	NAME.	BIRTH, Date and Place.	DEATH, Date and Place.	MARRIAGE, Date and Place.	TO WHOM MARRIED.	REMARKS.
247	James K. and Hetty Mauler Barber.					
658	Charles Barber.					
252	Charles T. and Margaret S. Kennedy Kellogg.					
659	Louisa W. Kellogg.					
254	Samuel D. and S. Louisa Kennedy Carpenter.					
†660	William Carpenter,		Deceased.			
661	Cora Carpenter.					
255	James M. and Mary Carter Kennedy.					
662	Henry S. Kennedy.					
†663	Robert Kennedy,		Deceased.			
664	William F. Kennedy.					
257	Edward and Ellen H. Kennedy Culbertson.					
†665	Lucy Culbertson,		March 3, 1849.			
666	Emma S. Culbertson,			Oct. 2, 1872.	Chauncey Ives,	Civil Engineer. Chambersburg, Pa.
667	Samuel D. Culbertson,				Not married.	
668	Nannie Purviance Culbertson			Oct. 19, 1876,	Daniel H. Wingert,	Attorney at Law. Reading, Pa.
669	James K. Culbertson,			April, 1877,	Nannie P. Armstrong.	
258	Joseph C. and Catherine Smith Kennedy.					
670	Thomas Kennedy,					Junction City, Kansas.
671	Margaret Kennedy,					Junction City, Kansas.
672	Henry Smith Kennedy,					Junction City, Kansas.
673	Emma Kennedy,					Junction City, Kansas.
674	Elizabeth Kennedy,					Junction City, Kansas.
675	Ariana Kennedy,					Junction City, Kansas.

No.	NAME.	BIRTH, Date and Place.	DEATH, Date and Place.	MARRIAGE, Date and Place.	TO WHOM MARRIED.	REMARKS.
676	Ellen Kennedy,					Junction City, Kansas.
677	Jane Patience Kennedy,					Junction City, Kansas.
678	Mary Kennedy,					Junction City, Kansas.
259	THOMAS B. and ARIANA STUART RIDDLE KENNEDY.					
679	John Stuart Kennedy,					Chambersburg, Pa.
680	Mary Margaret Kennedy,					Chambersburg, Pa.
681	Moorhead Cowell Kennedy,					Chambersburg, Pa.
682	James Riddle Kennedy,					Chambersburg, Pa.
683	Thos. Benjamin Kennedy,					Chambersburg, Pa.
684	Ariana Rebecca Kennedy,					Chambersburg, Pa.
260	WILLIAM L. and EMMELINE KENNEDY CHAMBERS.					
685	Alice Armstrong Chambers,			Oct. 26, 1871.	Theodore McGowan.	[Lawyer; Presb.; Repub. Chambersburg, Pa.
686	(Margaret Kennedy Chambers,					Chambersburg, Pa.
687	Ellen Chambers,					Chambersburg, Pa.
688	Carrie Chambers,					Chambersburg, Pa.
261	MAXWELL and MARTHA ORR KENNEDY.					
689	James Kennedy,					Junction City, Kansas.
690	Thomas Kennedy,					Junction City, Kansas.
691	John Kennedy,					Junction City, Kansas.
692	Frank Kennedy,					Junction City, Kansas.
693	Hetty Kennedy,					Junction City, Kansas.
694	Margaret Kennedy,					Junction City, Kansas.
262	JAMES and EMMA GRAY KENNEDY.					
695	Gray Kennedy,					Junction City, Kansas.
696	Guy Kennedy,					Junction City, Kansas.

No.	NAME.	BIRTH. Date and Place.	DEATH. Date and Place.	MARRIAGE. Date and Place.	TO WHOM MARRIED.	REMARKS.
697	William Kennedy, . . .	. . .	. . .	. . .	. . .	Junction City, Kansas.
698	Mary Emma Kennedy, . .	. . .	. . .	. . .	. . .	Junction City, Kansas.
266	Wychoff and Wife.					
699	Harry Wychoff, . . .	. . .	. . .	. . .	. . .	Junction City, Kansas.
700	Walter Wychoff, . . .	. . .	. . .	. . .	. . .	Junction City, Kansas.
701	Kate Wychoff, . . .	. . .	. . .	. . .	. . .	Junction City, Kansas.
267	J. Craig and Sarah Kennedy McLanahan.					
†702	{ Stewart Kennedy McLanahan, ... }	. . .	Died in infancy.			
703	Samuel McLanahan, . .	Feb. 12, 1853,	. . .	Oct. 11, 1877,	Maud Imbrie. . .	{ Presb. Preacher; Grad. Princeton : Republican. Baltimore, Md.
268	James Ferguson and Louisa Weiss McKinley Kennedy.					
704	Daniel M. Kennedy, . .	April 8, 1853,	. . .	Dec. 25, 1879,	Sue Shields, . .	Chambersburg, Pa.
705	James Stewart Kennedy, .	Oct. 27, 1856,	. . .	. . .	. . .	Chambersburg, Pa.
269	Edward A. and Matilda Kennedy Lesley.					
†706	James Lesley, ...	. . .	Died in infancy,			Chambersburg, Pa.
707	Nellie Lesley, ...	. . .	. . .	. . .	. . .	Chambersburg, Pa.
†708	May Lesley, ...	. . .	Died in infancy,			Chambersburg, Pa.
709	Florence Carroll Lesley, .	. . .	. . .	. . .	. . .	Chambersburg, Pa.
710	Edward Lesley, . . .	. . .	. . .	. . .	. . .	Chambersburg, Pa.
711	Edith Stewart Lesley, . .	. . .	. . .	. . .	. . .	Chambersburg, Pa.
272	William Kennedy and his 2d wife's children.					
712	Stewart Kennedy, . . .	. . .	. . .	. . .	. . .	Chambersburg, Pa.
713	William Kennedy, . . .	. . .	. . .	. . .	. . .	Chambersburg, Pa.
714	Helen Kennedy, . . .	. . .	. . .	. . .	. . .	Chambersburg, Pa.

No.	NAME	BIRTH. Date and Place.	DEATH. Date and Place.	MARRIAGE. Date and Place.	TO WHOM MARRIED.	REMARKS.
273	Henry and Sarah Jane Kennedy Reeves.					
715	Bessie Reeves, . . .			Married.		Gloucester, N. J.
716	P. Kennedy Reeves, . . .					Gloucester, N. J.
717	Charles Fithian Reeves,					Gloucester, N. J.
718	W. H. Green Reeves, .					Gloucester, N. J.
719	Henry Reeves, . . .					Gloucester, N. J.
720	Arthur Erwin Reeves, .					Gloucester, N. J.
721	Anna Robeson Reeves, .					Gloucester, N. J.
274	William and Margaret Van Buskirk Kennedy.					
722	John Henry Kennedy.					
723	(Sarah Van Buskirk Kennedy.)					
724	Daniel Stewart Kennedy.					
725	Hattie Sharp Kennedy.					
277	Edwin F. and Emma Kennedy Brewster.					
726	Lizzie R. Brewster.					
727	Ellen Thomson Brewster.					
728	Emma Kennedy Brewster.					
280	John F. and Mary Bell K. Kennedy.					
729	Henry R. Kennedy, . .					Bloomsbury, N. J.
730	Phineas B. Kennedy, . .					Bloomsbury, N. J. See 520.
283	W. H. and Elizabeth Hayes Green.					
731	Mary Elizabeth Green. . .	Oct. 30, 1859.		Dec. 7, 1880.	William Libbey, Jr.,	Professor; Presb. Princeton, N. J.
732	Helen Hayes Green, . .	June 13, 1864.				

No.	NAME.	BIRTH, Date and Place.	DEATH, Date and Place.	MARRIAGE, Date and Place.	TO WHOM MARRIED.	REMARKS.
284	JOHN THOMAS and SARAH ELIZABETH GREEN DUFFIELD.					
733	George Howard Duffield,	April 9, 1834.	July 11, 1857.	May 21, 1877.	Katherine North Greenleaf	Princeton, N. J. Presbyterian.
734	Anna Cora Duffield,	May 11, 1836.				Princeton, N. J. Presbyterian.
735	John Fletcher Duffield,	Dec. 9, 1857.				Princeton, N. J. Presbyterian.
736	Henry Green Duffield,	August 16, 1859.				Princeton, N. J. Presbyterian.
737	Helen Kennedy Duffield,	April 2, 1862.				Princeton, N. J. Presbyterian.
738	Sarah Green Duffield,	May 8, 1866.				Princeton, N. J. Presbyterian.
739	Edward Dickinson Duffield,	March 3, 1871.				Princeton, N. J. Presbyterian.
285	ANNA CORILLA GREEN. 1 h. E. D. YEOMANS. 2 h. MINOT S. MORGAN.					
740	George Green Yeomans,	Jan. 11, 1860.				Princeton, N. J. Presbyterian.
741	Anna L. Yeomans,	Nov. 21, 1861.				Princeton, N. J. Presbyterian.
742	Elizabeth L. Yeomans,	Feb. 28, 1868.				Princeton, N. J. Presbyterian.
743	Margaret S. Morgan,	Sept. 12, 1871.				Princeton, N. J. Presbyterian.
744	Minot C. Morgan,	Sept. 17, 1876.	Sept. 13, 1871.			Princeton, N. J. Presbyterian.
286	EDWARD T. GREEN, 1st and 2d WIFE.					
745	Walter Davenport Green,	July 24, 1864.				Trenton, N. J.
746	Anne Higbee Green,	Aug. 17, 1866.				Trenton, N. J.
747	Charlotte Beasley Green,	July 17, 1870.				Trenton, N. J.
288	ASA DUNAM and ALMINA FISHER CHRISTIAN.					
748	Valentine Christian,				Married; has two children.	Kansas.
749	Clementine Christian,				Married,	Kansas.
750	Alvina Christian,				Mr. Ganwood,	Kansas.
751	Edward Christian,				Unmarried.	
752	Robert Christian,				Unmarried.	
753	Uzel Christian,				Unmarried.	
754	Elsy Christian,				Unmarried.	
755	Martha Christian,				Unmarried.	

No.	NAME.	BIRTH, Date and Place.	DEATH, Date and Place.	MARRIAGE, Date and Place.	TO WHOM MARRIED.	REMARKS.
756	Irena Christian,				Unmarried.	
757	Byram Christian,				Unmarried.	
758	William Christian,				Unmarried.	
759	Herbert Christian,				Unmarried.	
308	CHARLES JOHNSTON KENNEDY, 1st and 2d WIFE.					
760	Frank Kennedy.					
761	Charles Kennedy.					
762	William Kennedy.					
763	Benton Kennedy.					
764	Jas. McWilliams Kennedy.					California.
312	WILLIAM H. and ELLEN PERLING KENNEDY.					
765	Carrie May Kennedy,					Lexington, Ill.
766	Margaret Kennedy,					Lexington, Ill.
767	Eddie Kennedy,					Lexington, Ill.
768	James Stewart Kennedy,					Lexington, Ill.
314	DANIEL and LETITIA K. SHAFFER.					
769	Ella Shaffer,					Michigan.
770	Robert Shaffer,					Michigan.
771	David Shaffer,					Michigan.
772	Arthur Shaffer,					Michigan.
773	Horace Shaffer,					Michigan.
774	Charles Shaffer,					Michigan.
318	AISSIA and SARAH ANN KENNEDY WELLS.					
775	Harry Wells,					South Bend, Ind.

No.	NAME.	BIRTH, Date and Place.	DEATH, Date and Place.	MARRIAGE, Date and Place.	TO WHOM MARRIED.	REMARKS.
319	SAMUEL P. and FRANCES A. DRAY KENNEDY.					
776	Caroline J. Kennedy, - - -	May 25, 1853,	. . . . .	April 6, 1879,	Albert Blanchard, - -	Ulm, Minn.
777	Clinton M. Kennedy, - -	Dec. 8, 1857.				
778	John W. Kennedy, - - -	Feb. 26, 1861.				
779	Ida May Kennedy, - - -	April 18, 1863.				
319½	RANDALL and MARY JANE KENNEDY SIMMONS.					
780	Laura Amanda Simmons, - -	April 29, 1849.				
781	Albert M. Simmons, - - -	Dec. 14, 1854.				
782	Robert E. Simmons, - - -	Nov. 15, 1864.				
320	ADALINE KENNEDY. 1 h. JOHN WISE. 2 h. P. H. McDERMID.					
783	Hugh M. McDermid, - - -	Sept. 12, 1858.				
784	Helen M. McDermid, - - -	Jan. 13, 1860.				
785	Albert Angers McDermid, - -	Sept. 14, 1862.				
786	Mary H. McDermid, - - -	June 20, 1865.				
320½	ISAAC and AMANDA B. KENNEDY HEATON.					
787	Mary L. Heaton, - - - -	Jan. 7, 1857,	. . . . .	Feb. 20, 1878.	Frank L. Daniels, - -	Bureau, Ill.
788	S. Austa Heaton, - - -	Mar. 27, 1859.	. . . . .	. . . .	. . . . .	Bureau, Ill.
789	Robt. Montgomery Heaton,	Sept. 26, 1866.	. . . . .	. . . .	. . . . .	Bureau, Ill.
790	George W. Heaton, - - -	Nov. 21, 1868.	. . . . .	. . . .	. . . . .	
321	JOEL B. and MARGARET BOYES KENNEDY.					
791	Lauson J. Kennedy, - - -	Dec. 18, 1854,	. . . . .	. . . .	. . . . .	Marion, Iowa.
792	Edward M. Kennedy, - -	Sept. 26, 1857,	. . . . .	. . . .	. . . . .	Minnesota.
793	Clarence D. M. Kennedy, -	Jan. 19, 1860,	. . . . .	. . . .	. . . . .	Minnesota.

No.	NAME.	BIRTH, Date and Place.	DEATH, Date and Place.	MARRIAGE, Date and Place.	TO WHOM MARRIED.	REMARKS.
323	FRANCIS MARION and JERUSHIA E. POST KENNEDY.					
794	Francis Marion Kennedy,	Jan. 7, 1837,				Howland, Ohio.
795	Jerushia E. Kennedy,	April 10, 1843,				
796	Lucy Mariette Kennedy,	March 26, 1865,				Minnesota.
797	Austa E. Kennedy,	May 11, 1867,				Minnesota.
798	Frances Mildred Kennedy,	Aug. 16, 1869,				Minnesota.
799	Robert Bruce Kennedy,	Nov. 16, 1872,				
800	Arthur James Kennedy,	April 30, 1877.				
325	EDWARD J. and AUSTA C. KENNEDY BOYES.					
801	Ralph M. Boyes, ⎫ (twins)	April 27, 1860,				Minnesota.
802	Frank E. Boyes, ⎭					
803	Mary Elizabeth Boyes,	Sept. 21, 1862.				
326	GUSTAVUS and MARY JANE KING WILSON.					
804	M. R. Wilson,					Warren, Ohio.
805	Emily Wilson,					Warren, Ohio.
327	S. S. and ABIGAIL CHAMBERLAIN KING.					
806	Ralph King,	July 15, 1848,				Howland, Ohio.
807	Jennie B. King,	Sept. 28, 1856,		Nov. 29, 1876,	John S. Kennedy,	Howland, Ohio.
808	James Bliss King,					Howland, Ohio.
809	William King.					
328	SAMUEL and ELIZABETH SUTLIFF KING.					
810	Darwin King.					
811	Alice King.					
812	Carrie King.					

No.	NAME	BIRTH, Date and Place	DEATH, Date and Place	MARRIAGE, Date and Place	TO WHOM MARRIED	REMARKS
329	Edward and Caroline King Delas.					
813	Charles K. Delin,					Howland, Ohio.
814	Bliss K. Delin.					
330	James and Amanda King Phillips.					
815	Melissa Phillips.					
816	Irene Phillips.					
331	James and Olive King Wilson.					
817	Amine Wilson,	Nov. 18, 1838,	July 1, 1863,	Oct. 4, 1857,	Byron Taylor,	Bazetta, Ohio. Farmer.
818	William W. Wilson,	July 11, 1840,	Sept. 28, 1844,	Nov. 2, 1868,	Mahala Slarner,	Bazetta, Ohio. Farmer.
819	James B. Wilson,	Sept. 3, 1843,	May 30, 1863,			Bazetta, Ohio.
820	Samuel H. Wilson,	Dec. 30, 1849,		March 24, 1875,	Adelia Gibson,	Bazetta, Ohio. Farmer.
821	Ovid O. Wilson,	Oct. 24, 1852,		March 22, 1876,	Julia Dougherty,	Bazetta, Ohio. Farmer.
822	Thomas K. Wilson,	Jan. 12, 1855,				Howland, Ohio. Farmer.
334	Stots L. and Jane K. King Abell.					
823	Ada Abell,				Silas Davis,	
824	Roda Abell,				A. Mason.	
825	Lathrop Abell.					
826	William Abell.					
337	James F. and Cornelia Andrews King.					
827	Kate King,	Oct. 10, 1863,				
828	Elmire A. King,	Nov. 30, 1865,				
339	William and Anna Orilla King Chamberlain.					
829	Frank King,	March 23, 1849,		April 16, 1872,	Abbie Rogers,	Republican.
830	Mary King,	May 8, 1850,				
831	Charles W. King,	March 19, 1860,				

No.	NAME.	BIRTH, Date and Place.	DEATH, Date and Place.	MARRIAGE, Date and Place.	TO WHOM MARRIED.	REMARKS.
340	CHARLES R. and JERUSHA KING HUNT.					
832	William C. Hunt, ...	Nov. 10, 1853.				Doctor.
833	Charles K. Hunt, ...	Dec. 25, 1856.				
341	WILLIAM H. and PERMELIA KENNEDY MILLER.					
834	Addison F. Miller, . . .	Oct. 4, 1860.				Bazetta, Ohio. Artist.
835	Clarence P. Miller, . . .	July 11, 1866.				
836	Azalia Belle Miller, . . .	July 22, 1869.				
837	Phelps Lloyd Miller, . . .	Jan. 13, 1876.				
342	PHLANDER and ELIZA A. CHUSEY KENNEDY.					
838	Minnie A. Kennedy, . . .	April 22, 1870.				
839	Maud Irene Kennedy, . . .	Nov. 6, 1876.				
840	Jennie Belle Kennedy, . . .	Dec. 6, 1878.				
345	AYLINER B. and LUCY C. KENNEDY McCLEARY.					
841	Merle Adelia McCleary, . . .	August 2, 1875.				
842	Harry McCleary, . . .	May 22, 1877.				
346	ANTHONY WAYNE and EU-NICE KELLOGG KENNEDY.					
843	Mary Kennedy, . . .	August 15, 1873.				
347	KENNEDY and ANN TODNGS KENNEDY ANDREWS.					
844	William F. Andrews, . . .	Nov. 22, 1868.				
845	Gertrude Andrews, . . .	Nov. 20, 1878.				

No.	NAME.	BIRTH, Date and Place.	DEATH, Date and Place.	MARRIAGE, Date and Place.	TO WHOM MARRIED.	REMARKS.
348	Cassius Clay and Alice Kellogg Kennedy.					
846	Lloyd B. Kennedy, . . .	Dec. 7, 1870.				
847	Carl W. Kennedy, . . .	April 20, 1874.				
350	William W. and Sallie A. Sowers Kennedy.					
†848	Jessie Kennedy, . . .	Aug. 5, 1863.	March 28, 1879.			
351	George W. and Eliza Bailey Kennedy.					
849	James F. Kennedy, . . .	April 5, 1868.				
352	James L. and Betsy Alderman Kennedy.					
850	Charles H. Kennedy, . .	Dec. 29, 1872.				
353	John S. and Jessie B. King Kennedy.					
†851	Freddie M. Kennedy, . .	March 22, 1878.	March 17, 1879.			
354	Francis N. and Esther Ann Kennedy Andrews.					
†852	Daniel F. Andrews, . .	Sept. 11, 1857,	Feb. 10, 1859.			
†853	Annie Eveline Andrews,	Nov. 15, 1860,	April 25, 1866.			
854	Linda Esther Andrews,	Oct. 13, 1867.				
355	Henry H. and Clara Harding Kennedy.					
855	Harding M. Kennedy, . .	Dec. 28, 1870,			. . .	Goodyear's Bar, Cal.
856	Ellis C. Kennedy, . . .	Sept. 2, 1873,			. . .	Goodyear's Bar, Cal.
857	Laura E. Kennedy, . . .	Nov. 27, 1875,			. . .	Goodyear's Bar, Cal.

No.	NAME.	BIRTH, Date and Place.	DEATH, Date and Place.	MARRIAGE, Date and Place.	TO WHOM MARRIED.	REMARKS.
356	Morris C. and Selma Reel Kennedy.					
858	Arlington R. Kennedy, . .	April 6, 1873.				Cleveland, Ohio.
857	Edwin Boyd and Fannie M. Terry Kennedy.					
859	Florence E. Kennedy, . .	Dec. 2, 1877.				
860	Lewis Maxwell Kennedy.	Feb. 9, 1880.				Warren, Ohio.
358	M. E. and Helen M. Kennedy Halstead.					
861	Ethel E. Halstead.	March 12, 1877,				Howland, Ohio.
360	William W. and Addie Ewing Kennedy.					
862	Samuel Ewing Kennedy, .	August 6, 1878.				
363	George and Bertha McClurg Anderson.					
862½	George Anderson.					
862½	Anna Belle Anderson.					
364	Mr. Cromwell and Harriet Anderson.					
862½	Harriet Cromwell.				Ross Stanley.	
368	Richard M. Bear. 1 w. Mary McDowell. 2 w. Eliza J. Tait. 3 w. no issue.					
863	Emma J. Bear, . . .	May, 1847,		April, 1866,	R. H. Bear.	
†864	John Jacob Bear,	August, 1850,	March, 1872.	1866,		
865	Martha Ellen Bear,	Feb., 1852,				New York.
866	William C. Bear, . .	Oct., 1853,				Lawyer. Johnstown, Pa.

No.	NAME.	BIRTH, Date and Place.	DEATH, Date and Place.	MARRIAGE, Date and Place.	TO WHOM MARRIED.	REMARKS.
867	Harry Bear,	1865,				
†868	Richard Charles Bear,	1868,	1874.			
369	**WILLIAM M. BEAR.** 1 w. MARY S. SHARP. 2 w. MARY S. CLARK.					
869	Richard H. Bear,	July 10, 1841,		April, 1866,	Emma Jane Bear.	Erie, Pa. Mail Agent.
†870	Leonidas Hamline Bear,	July 16, 1846,	Jan., 1847.			
871	Mary Williamina Bear,	June 7, 1848,		1869,	C. A. Shriver,	Farmer, Abeline, Kansas.
872	Edmund James Bear,	June 26, 1850,				
873	Jane Margaret Bear,	April 29, 1852,		Nov. 4, 1873,	Benj. F. Thurber.	Worthington, Minn. Maj. in the Army.
†874	Martha Emily Bear,	May 21, 1854,	Aug. 16, 1861.			Bigelow, Minn.
†875	William Jacob Bear,	Feb. 21, 1856,	Jan. 11, 1868.			
876	Lizzie Newell Bear,	Jan. 1, 1857,				Bigelow, Minn.
†877	Ellen May Bear,	Sept. 14, 1867,				
370	**CYRUS and ELLEN A. BEAR CLARK.**					
878	Martha Ella Clark,	1849,	1870,		—— Ries.	
372	**CHAS. WESLEY and ANNA PANCAKE BEAR.**					
879	Alfred Cookman Bear,					New Castle, Pa.
880	Martha Ella Bear,					New Castle, Pa.
376	**JAS. KENNEDY and MARIA GALLY BEAR.**					
881	Charles Garroway Bear,	1863.				
882	Ella Bear.					
883	Eva Bear.					
377	**ANNA ELIZABETH COWNICK.** 1 h. PIERSON BATES. 2 h. THOMAS JEFFERSON PHILLIS.					
884	Clarissa Jane Bates,	Jan. 4, 1810,		Feb. 5, 1867,	Cyrus S. Bowman,	Lawyer; Mayor of Bryan, Ohio.

No.	NAME.	BIRTH, Date and Place.	DEATH, Date and Place.	MARRIAGE, Date and Place.	TO WHOM MARRIED.	REMARKS.
885	Horner Phillis, ...	June 18, 1851,	. . . .	Feb. 24, 1871,	Frances Hoover, . .	Dentist. Bryan. Ohio.
886	Mary Phillis, ...	July 18, 1853,	. . . .	June 27, 1876,	Curtis Beechler, . .	
382	Maxwell Kennedy and Mary Heberton Moorhead.					Manufacturer: Presb.; Rep. Pitts.
†887	Lizzie H. Moorhead, .	June 16, 1856.	. . . .	June 1, 1878,	John W. Watt. . . .	
888	Jennie Logan Moorhead, .	July 18, 1858.				
387	Wm. Jefferson and Emily B. Black Moorhead.					
889	Lizzie Butler Moorhead,	Feb. 13, 1866,	. . . .	. . . .	. . . .	Pittsburgh, Pa.
890	James Kennedy Moorhead,	Feb. 29, 1868,	. . . .	. . . .	. . . .	Pittsburgh, Pa.
891	Saml. W. Black Moorhead,	Jan. 14, 1870,	. . . .	. . . .	. . . .	Pittsburgh, Pa.
†892	Helen Moorhead, . .	Oct. 25, 1872,	Jan. 25, 1878,	. . . .	. . . .	Pittsburgh, Pa.
893	Maxwell K. Moorhead, . .	July 14, 1877,	. . . .	. . . .	. . . .	Pittsburgh, Pa.
389	Jas. B. and Jessie Adaline Moorhead Murdock.					
894	Jas. K. Moorhead Murdock,	Mar. 3, 1869,	. . . .	. . . .	. . . .	Pittsburgh, Pa.
895	John Murdock, . . .	July 28, 1872,	. . . .	. . . .	. . . .	Pittsburgh, Pa.
896	Florence Murdock, . .	Dec. 18, 1877,	. . . .	. . . .	. . . .	Pittsburgh, Pa.
897	Wm. Moorhead Murdock, .	June 1, 1878,	. . . .	. . . .	. . . .	Pittsburgh, Pa.
390	Charles Illross and Lucy Phelps Hickman Moorhead.					
898	Joel Barlow Moorhead, . .	Sept. 3, 1871.	. . . .			Montgomery Co., Pa.
391	George Clifford and Ada Elizabeth Moorhead Thomas.					
899	Bessie Moorhead Thomas,	Oct. 24, 1869,	. . . .			Philadelphia.
900	George C. Thomas, . .	Oct. 3, 1873,	May 31, 1875,			Philadelphia.

No.	NAME.	BIRTH, Date and Place.	DEATH, Date and Place.	MARRIAGE, Date and Place.	TO WHOM MARRIED.	REMARKS.
901	Sophy Thomas,	Feb. 7, 1876,				Philadelphia.
902	Leonard M. Thomas,	May 27, 1878,				Philadelphia.
392	JAY and CLARA ALICE MOORHEAD COOKE.					
903	Caroline Clara Cooke,	Aug. 29, 1870,				Philadelphia.
904	Jay Cooke,	April 22, 1872,				Philadelphia.
393	JOSEPH EARLSTON and CAROLINE FRANCES MOORHEAD THROPP.					
905	Joseph Earlston Thropp,	Feb. 10, 1874,				Montgomery Co., Pa.
906	Clara Moorhead Thropp,	Oct. 22, 1875.				
907	Amy Smith Thropp,	Sept. 7, 1878.				
396	HENRY HENLY and YSIDORA BEATRICE MOORHEAD DODGE.					
908	William Chapman Dodge,	July 23, 1875,				Washington, D. C.
909	Frances Henly Dodge,	Sept. 28, 1876,				Washington, D. C.
910	Sarah Esther Dodge,	July 19, 1879,				Washington, D. C.
399	S. L. and EMILY R. MONTGOMERY RUSSEL.					
911	Montgomery Russel,					Bedford, Pa.
†912	Eliza M. Russel,		Deceased,			Bedford, Pa.
†913	Isabel Russel,		Deceased,			Bedford, Pa.
914	Florence E. Russel,					Bedford, Pa.
915	Eleanor Russel,					Bedford, Pa.
916	Samuel M. Russel,					Bedford, Pa.
400	JAMES B. MONTGOMERY. 1 w. RACH. ANTHONY. 2 w. MARY PHELPS.					
917	Henry Montgomery.					
918	Mary Montgomery.					

No.	NAME.	BIRTH, Date and Place.	DEATH, Date and Place.	MARRIAGE, Date and Place.	TO WHOM MARRIED.	REMARKS.
919	Antoinette Montgomery.					
920	Phelps Montgomery.					
921	Eliza Montgomery.					
922	Constance Montgomery.					
923	Russel Montgomery.					
402	T. S. and Sarah E. Montgomery Minor.					Port Townsend, Washington Ter. Port Townsend, Washington Ter.
924	Elizabeth Minor,					
925	Judith S. Minor,					
404	James and Ada J. Montgomery McCrea.					
926	James A. McCrea,					Philadelphia.
927	Archibald McCrea,					Philadelphia.
410	Samuel E. and Mary Letitia Kennedy Webster.					Washington, N. Jersey.
928	Mary Kennedy Webster,	Dec. 19, 1875,				
929	Hellen Burress Webster,	Dec. 5, 1876,				
930	Samuel Kennedy Webster,	June 13, 1878.				
411	Henry Martyn and Mary E. Jacobs Kennedy.					
931	William Jacobs Kennedy..	Nov. 12, 1877.				
413	Fred. C. and Emma Kennedy Green Lewis.					
932	Edith K. Lewis,	Sept. 15, 1870.				
933	Geo. Smith Green Lewis,	May 22, 1875.				
422	Herbert Morris and Arabella Berk Kennedy.					
933	Maxwell King Kennedy.					

No.	NAME.	BIRTH, Date and Place.	DEATH, Date and Place.	MARRIAGE, Date and Place.	TO WHOM MARRIED.	REMARKS.
924	Sibilla Kennedy,					
925	Sarah Kennedy,					Danvers, Ill.
426	Edward W. and Mary Elizabeth Martin Barnes.					
936	Jessie K. Barnes,	Jan. 13, 1866,				Delphi, Ind.
937	Lewis M. Barnes,	Jan. 28, 1869,	Feb. 18, 1869,			Delphi, Ind.
938	Harry K. Barnes,	Jan. 28, 1869,	August 28, 1870,			Delphi, Ind.
939	Mary Emma Barnes,	Oct. 25, 1870,	March 11, 1879,			Delphi, Ind.
940	Mabel C. Barnes,	May 1, 1872,	Feb. 28, 1879,			Delphi, Ind.
941	Charles E. Barnes,	May 13, 1878,	April 26, 1879,			Delphi, Ind.
942	George Edwin Barnes,	March 23, 1880,				Delphi, Ind.
427	A. P. and Emma Bell Martin Cory.					
943	Luella B. Cory,	Nov. 13, 1869,	March 29, 1876,			Danvers, Ill.
944	Mary A. Cory,	June 21, 1871,				Danvers, Ill.
945	Lewis M. Cory,	Nov. 17, 1872,	Oct. 22, 1880,			Danvers, Ill.
946	Agnes K. Cory,	July 2, 1875,				Danvers, Ill.
947	Edith E. Cory,	Nov. 17, 1876,				Danvers, Ill.
948	Leroy Davidson Cory,	Oct. 5, 1878,				Danvers, Ill.
433	Robert Henry Clay and Alice Kennedy Hill.					
949	Howard Kennedy Hill,	Feb. 2, 1879.				Philadelphia.
9491	Alice Hill,	May 13, 1881.				
443	George Bryan and Fanny Grant Lyon Logan.					
950	David Elliott Logan,	Jan. 22, 1871,	June 7, 1871,			Presbyterian. Pittsburgh.
951	John T. Logan,	July 2, 1872,				Presbyterian. Pittsburgh.
952	Patton Lyon Logan,	April 30, 1874,				Presbyterian. Pittsburgh.
953	Archibald Hodge Logan,	June 25, 1877,				Presbyterian. Pittsburgh.
954	Alice Lyon Logan,	June 24, 1879,				Presbyterian. Pittsburgh.

No.	NAME.	BIRTH, DATE AND PLACE.	DEATH, DATE AND PLACE.	MARRIAGE, DATE AND PLACE.	TO WHOM MARRIED.	REMARKS.
444	Edward Payson and Anna Clark Logan.					
955	Edna Logan, ...	Nov. 19, 1871.	. . . .	. . . .	. . . .	Presbyterian. Pittsburgh.
956	Mary Clark Logan, . .	May 11, 1877.	. . . .	. . . .	. . . .	Presbyterian. Pittsburgh.
957	James Clark Logan, .	Dec. 16, 1878.	. . . .	. . . .	. . . .	Presbyterian. Pittsburgh.
446	Thomas Dale and Carrie B. Mahoney Logan.					
958	Howard Logan, . . .	Jan. 7, 1878.	. . . .	. . . .	. . . .	Presbyterian. Pittsburgh.
447	Charles Hodge and Henrietta Bryan Logan Scott.					
959	William McKendry Scott, .	Oct. 18, 1876.				
960	Samuel Bryan Scott, .	August 28, 1878.				
449	Charles T. and Elizabeth T. Boyd Stewart.					
961	Elizabeth L. Stewart, .	Sept. 9, 1846.	. . . .	Oct. 5, 1869.	George N. West. . . .	Bath, Maine.
962	William Stewart, . . .	Feb. 5, 1850.				
963	Robert Henry Stewart, .	Nov. 17, 1854.	1855.			
964	Mary Alice Stewart, . .	Dec. 6, 1868.	1868.			
965	Charles Stewart, . . .	March 3, 1872.				
450	John Logan and Agnes Copeland Boyd.					
966	William C. Boyd, . .	Nov. 6, 1864.	Died young,			Allegheny City, Pa.
967	John Logan Boyd, . .	Nov. 20, 1866.	. . . .			Allegheny City, Pa.
968	Henrietta Logan Boyd, .	Sept. 10, 1870.	. . . .			Allegheny City, Pa.
969	Maxwell Moorhead Boyd, .	May 5, 1872.	. . . .			Allegheny City, Pa.
451	Henry and Harriet Cline Boyd.					
970	William Boyd, ...	Dec. 31, 1864.				Washington, New Jersey.

No.	NAME.	BIRTH, Date and Place.	DEATH, Date and Place.	MARRIAGE, Date and Place.	TO WHOM MARRIED.	REMARKS.
451	Edward Boyd,	August 8, 1866,				
†452	Ann C. Boyd,	May 25, 1871,	August 20, 1871.			
452	ADAM W. and MARY JANE BOYD BOWMAN.					
†973	William H. Bowman,	May 5, 1857,	July 2, 1858,			Washington, New Jersey.
974	John Logan Bowman,	June 7, 1859,				Washington, New Jersey.
975	Samuel Thomas Bowman,	Oct. 11, 1862,				Washington, New Jersey.
976	Lambert M. Bowman,	June 10, 1866,				Washington, New Jersey.
977	Mary Elizabeth Bowman,	Dec. 25, 1868,				Washington, New Jersey.
978	Ed. Bryan Bowman,	Sept. 1, 1873,				Washington, New Jersey.
453	WILLIAM H. and SARAH H. JAMES BOYD.					
979	Elizabeth J. Boyd,	Feb. 2, 1868,				Burlington, New Jersey.
980	Mary L. Boyd,	Feb. 3, 1870,				
981	Fanny Chester Boyd,	Dec. 20, 1872,				
982	Frederick Root Boyd,	Feb. 10, 1874,				
983	Alexander James Boyd,	Feb. 13, 1876,				
984	Rebecca James Boyd,	March 2, 1879,				
454	SAMUEL E. and NANCY C. BOYD CRAFT.					
985	Alexander Jamison Craft,	April 21, 1864,				
986	James Boyd Craft,	August 31, 1866,				Washington, New Jersey.
987	Samuel Emlin Craft,	May 18, 1871,				
455	JAMES L. and LYDIA A. WASHING BOYD.					
†988	Catherine Boyd,	Nov. 3, 1870,	March 22, 1872,			Washington, New Jersey.
†989	Joseph G. Boyd,	Jan. 12, 1873,	Sept. 3, 1873,			Washington, New Jersey.
990	Cora N. Boyd,	August 3, 1875,				Washington, New Jersey.
†991	Lydia A. Boyd,	Feb. 16, 1879,	June 17, 1879,			Washington, New Jersey.

No.	NAME.	BIRTH, Date and Place.	DEATH, Date and Place.	MARRIAGE, Date and Place.	TO WHOM MARRIED.	REMARKS.
458	WILLIAM G. and HENRIETTA LOGAN BOYD CREVELING.					
992	William H. Creveling, . .	Sept. 10, 1878.				Washington, New Jersey.
459	MARGARETTA KENNEDY. 1 h. W. C. CARR. 2 h. S. D. KANE.					
993	Robert T. Kennedy Carr, .	August 27, 1855,				Pittsburgh, Pa.
994	Henry H. Carr, ...	July, 1863,				Pittsburgh, Pa.
995	Lillie Kane, ...	Oct, 1876,				Pittsburgh, Pa.
460	GEORGE and LILLIE E. KENNEDY SHIRAS.					
996	George Shiras, ...	Jan. 1, 1859,				Lawyer. Pittsburgh.
997	Winfield K. Shiras, . .	March 15, 1860.				Lawyer. Pittsburgh.
461	WILLIAM H. and EMMA L. KENNEDY FORSYTH.					
998	Lillie Shiras Forsyth, . .	Nov. 1, 1866,				Pittsburgh, Pa.
999	Russell Kennedy Forsyth, .	Oct. 4, 1869,				Pittsburgh, Pa.
1000	Margaret H. Forsyth, . .	Jan. 22, 1872,				Pittsburgh, Pa.
1001	Willa H. Forsyth, . . .	May 12, 1875,				Pittsburgh, Pa.
462	FRED. H. and KATE BROWN KENNEDY.					
1002	Robert T. Kennedy, . . .	March, 1869,				Pittsburgh, Pa.
1003	Sarah M. G. Kennedy, . .	May, 1872,				Pittsburgh, Pa.
463	WILLIAM R. and ALICE MARY KENNEDY HOWE.					
1004	Bessie C. Howe, ...	March 21, 1866,				Pittsburgh, Pa.
1005	Florence Howe, ...	March 29, 1877,				Pittsburgh, Pa.

No.	NAME.	BIRTH, Date and Place.	DEATH, Date and Place.	MARRIAGE, Date and Place.	TO WHOM MARRIED.	REMARKS.
464	William M. and Eliza McClintock Kennedy.					
1006	Frank W. Kennedy, . . .	Jan. 1876,				Pittsburgh, Pa.
1006½	Walter McClintock Kennedy	August 30, 1880.				Pittsburgh, Pa.
465	C. H. and Bessie E. Kennedy Call.					
1007	Jennie K. Call, . . .	Nov. 15, 1876,				Marquette, Mich.
1008	Saidee W. Call, . . .	May 30, 1879,				Marquette, Mich.
466	F. B. and Sara S. Kennedy Speer.					
1009	Frank B. Speer, . . .	May 2, 1872,				
1010	Philip Speer, . . .	April 21, 1874.				
469	J. G. and Jennie M. K. Reynolds.					
1010½	Henry C. Reynolds, . .	Oct. 5, 1880.				
471	John Matthias and Florence Graddy Kennedy.					
1011	Willie Kennedy, . . .					A daughter, Lancaster Co., Pa.
1012	Jessie Kennedy, . . .					Lancaster Co., Pa.
1013	Winfield Scott Kennedy,					Lancaster Co., Pa.
1014	Graddy Kennedy, . . .					Lancaster Co., Pa.
473	Seth Patterson and Margaret Maxwell Kennedy Buyers.					
1015	Edgar Stanley Buyers, . .	Sept., 1878,				Lancaster Co., Pa.
479	David and Anna Margaret Kennedy Marquis.					
1016	John Logan Marquis, . .	August 21, 1861,				Pittsburgh, Pa.

No.	NAME.	BIRTH, DATE AND PLACE.	DEATH, DATE AND PLACE.	MARRIAGE, DATE AND PLACE.	TO WHOM MARRIED.	REMARKS.
1017	Lydia Marquis,	Dec. 16, 1866,	. . . .	. . . .	. . . .	Pittsburgh, Pa.
1018	George Paull Marquis,	Sept. 11, 1868,	. . . .	. . . .	. . . .	Pittsburgh, Pa.
1019	Henrietta Logan Marquis,	May 14, 1870,	. . . .	. . . .	. . . .	Pittsburgh, Pa.
†1020	David Kennedy Marquis,	May 5, 1875,	Aug. 11, 1875.	. . . .	. . . .	Pittsburgh, Pa.
480	R. S. and JOSEPHINE Y. BUYERS McILVAINE.					
1021	Cora E. McIlvaine,	. . . .	. . . .	. . . .	. . . .	Lancaster Co., Pa.
1022	Winfield K. McIlvaine,	. . . .	. . . .	. . . .	. . . .	Lancaster Co., Pa.
1023	Jennie D. McIlvaine,	. . . .	. . . .	. . . .	. . . .	Lancaster Co., Pa.
481	W. D. and LETITIA A. BUYERS ROUNDS.					
1024	Josephine B. Rounds,	. . . .	. . . .	. . . .	. . . .	Lancaster Co., Pa.
1025	Charles D. Rounds,	. . . .	. . . .	. . . .	. . . .	Lancaster Co., Pa.
1026	William K. Rounds,	. . . .	. . . .	. . . .	. . . .	Lancaster Co., Pa.
484	EDWIN and MARGARETTA K. BUYERS EWING.					
1027	Albert Ewing.					
1028	Edwin Ewing.					
485	EDWARD and ELIZA READING REMINGTON.					
1029	Maria Remington.					
1030	Robert Remington.					
1031	Myra Remington.					
1032	Anna P. Remington.					
1033	Edward Remington.					
486	JOHN P. and MARY READING GRANDON.					
1034	Philip Grandon.					
1035	Robert R. Grandon.					

No.	NAME.	BIRTH, Date and Place.	DEATH, Date and Place.	MARRIAGE, Date and Place.	TO WHOM MARRIED.	REMARKS.
487	FRANK and *see* MISS HEPBURN READING.					
1036	Robert Reading.					
1037	Frank Reading.					
1038	Jane Reading.					
488	ALEXANDER and ELMIRA READING GULICK.					
1039	Myra Gulick.					
1040	Charlton Gulick.					
1011	Laura Gulick.					
1042	Arnot Gulick.					
491	HARRISON READING and WIFE.					
1043	—— Reading.					
493	JOHN READING and *see* MISS SCUDDER FARLEY.					
1044	Anna S. Farley.					
1045	Jacob Farley.					
1046	George Farley.					
1047	Isaac Farley.					
494	A. G. and ANNA FARLEY RICHEY.					
1048	Mary Richey.					
1049	Isaac Richey.					
1050	Lilly Richey.				Charles Fisk.	
495	GEORGE and *see* MISS ORDYKE FARLEY.					
1051	Elizabeth Farley.					

62

No.	NAME	BIRTH, Date and Place.	DEATH, Date and Place.	MARRIAGE, Date and Place.	TO WHOM MARRIED.	REMARKS.
498	—— Sloakum and his wife, nee Mary Graxims.					
1652	—— Sloakum.					
502	P. L. and Mary Scovel Senour.					
1053	Mary Senour,					Pittsburgh, Pa.
1051	Henrietta Senour,					Pittsburgh, Pa.
1055	Wm. Breckenridge Senour,					Pittsburgh, Pa.
1056	Ella Bradley Senour,				Charles Joy.	Pittsburgh, Pa.
1057	Bertha Senour,					Pittsburgh, Pa.
503	James M. and Mary Milford Scovel.					
1058	H. Sydney Scovel,					Lawyer, Camden, N. J.
1059	Annie D. Scovel,					Camden, N. J.
1060	Mary M. Scovel,					Camden, N. J.
504	Edward and Sallie Scovel Shields.					
1061	Clara J. Shields,					Cape May, N. J.
1062	Henry B. Shields,					Cape May, N. J.
1063	Hannah S. Shields,					Cape May, N. J.
1064	Eddie S. Shields,					Cape May, N. J.
1065	William H. Shields,					Cape May, N. J.
1066	Lilian M. Shields,					Cape May, N. J.
505	Sylvester F. and Caroline Woodruff Scovel.					
1067	Minor Scovel,	July 16, 1858,				Pittsburgh, Pa.
1068	Charles W. Scovel,	Aug. 17, 1862,				Pittsburgh, Pa.
1069	Amelia Scovel,	July 18, 1865,				Pittsburgh, Pa.
1070	Henry Sylvester Scovel,	July 29, 1869,				Pittsburgh, Pa.
1071	Elizabeth Benny Scovel,	March 8, 1876,				Pittsburgh, Pa.

No.	NAME.	BIRTH, Date and Place.	DEATH, Date and Place.	MARRIAGE, Date and Place.	TO WHOM MARRIED.	REMARKS.
506	CHARLES and HARRIET SCOVEL ALLING.					
1072	Albert Scovel Alling,					Madison, Ind.
1073	Kate Lodge Alling,					Madison, Ind.
1074	Charles Alling,					Madison, Ind.
1075	Howard S. Alling,					Madison, Ind.
1076	William R. Alling,					Madison, Ind.
1077	George Robinson Alling,					Madison, Ind.
1078	Van Wagenen Alling,					Madison, Ind.
1079	Fred. Page Alling,					Madison, Ind.
507	RICHARD and HANNAH SCOVEL MUZZY.					
1080	Caroline Muzzy,					Springfield, Ohio.
1081	Jane Muzzy,					Springfield, Ohio.
1082	Reeder Muzzy,					Springfield, Ohio.
508	KITTY SCOVEL and husband, BURROWES.					
1083	Harry Burrowes,					Franklin.
1084	Clifford Burrowes,					Franklin.
509	JAMES D. and BELLE SCOVEL BARNETT.					
1085	William Barnett,					Louisiana.
1086	Robert Barnett,					Louisiana.
1087	Earl Barnett,					Louisiana.
1088	Allen Barnett,					Louisiana.
510	ROBERT A. and CLARA COBB SCOVEL.					
1089	Louise Scovel,					Chicago, Ill.
518	GEORGE G. BROWNING and wife, nee Miss WHITE.					
1090	Eleanor Browning,					Camden, N. J.

No.	NAME.	BIRTH, DATE AND PLACE.	DEATH, DATE AND PLACE.	MARRIAGE, DATE AND PLACE.	TO WHOM MARRIED.	REMARKS.
520	JOHN FRELINGHUYSEN and MARY B. KENNEDY KENNEDY.					
1091	Henry R. Kennedy, Jr.,	April 4, 1865,				Bloomsburg, N. J.
1092	Phineas B. Kennedy,	June 13, 1867,				Bloomsburg, N. J.
522	ROBERT HEANRIE KENNEDY 1 w. ISABELLA WILLIAMSON. 2 w. RACHEL WARNE.					
1093	Miriam Kay Kennedy,	July 29, 1865.				
1094	Elizabeth La Grange Kennedy,	May 16, 1867.				
1095	Chas. F. Williamson Kennedy,	April 24, 1869.				
1096	Henry R. Kennedy,	May 3, 1871.				
	SECOND WIFE.					
1097	Frederick Frelinghuysen Kennedy,	Sept. 13, 1877.				
523	THEODORE FRELINGHUYSEN and MARY CARPENTER KENNEDY.					
1098	Grace Kennedy,	Sept. 13, 1872.				
524	THEODORE B. and BEULAH ELIZABETH KENNEDY HANCE.					
1099	Henry R. Kennedy Hance,	March 7, 1877.				
1100	Louise F. Kennedy Hance,	Nov. 24, 1879.				
526	DAVID and CATHERINE MARR McCORMICK.					
1101	Julia McCormick,					Harrisburg, Pa.

No.	NAME.	BIRTH, Date and Place.	DEATH, Date and Place.	MARRIAGE, Date and Place.	TO WHOM MARRIED.	REMARKS.
1102	Lizzie McCormick,					Harrisburg, Pa.
1103	Agnes McCormick,					One child. Harrisburg, Pa.
1104	Nellie McCormick,				Married,	Harrisburg, Pa.
1105	David M. McCormick,					Harrisburg, Pa.
531	J. Irvin and Harriet Marr Gregg.					
1106	Irvin Gregg,					Lewisburg, Pa.
1107	Robert Gregg,					Lewisburg, Pa.
532	James and Kate Knight Marr.					
1108			Deceased.			
1109			Deceased.			
1110						
1111						
1112						
533	Frank and M. Elizabeth M. Killernan.					
	Large family.					
534	J. Josephine Marr. 1 h. Donovan. 2 h. Geo. A. Breaux.					
1113	Daisy Donovan.					
535	Henry and Angeline Marr Knight.					
1114	Horace Knight,					Philadelphia.
1115	Joseph Knight,					Philadelphia.
541	Addson and Margaret Sheriff Marr.					
1116	William Marr.					

No.	NAME.	BIRTH, Date and Place.	DEATH, Date and Place.	MARRIAGE, Date and Place.	TO WHOM MARRIED.	REMARKS.
†1117 1118	Graham Marr, ... Phineas Marr.		Deceased.			
554	Dr. Guy and his wife, née Josepha Bowman.					
1119	Josepha Guy.					
558	Mr. Hegins and wife, née Henrietta Bowman.					
1120	Jesse Hughs.					
560	John A. and Anna Eliza Marr Grier.					
1121 1122 1123	Margaret J. Grier, . . Thomas Graham Grier, . Edward Robie Grier, . .	July 15, 1862, July 23, 1865, Sept. 1, 1869.		: : : : :	: : : : :	Philadelphia. Philadelphia. Philadelphia.
570 1124	James Marr.					
586	John Jason and M. A. B. Everett.					
1125 1126	C. E. Everett. W. C. Everett.					
588	William Felix and A. H. C. Bisel.					
1127 1128	W. C. Bisel. G. C. Bisel.					
589	Daniel L. and Mary S. Bisel.					
1129 1130	Kent H. Bisel. Anna L. Bisel.					

No.	NAME.	BIRTH, Date and Place.	DEATH, Date and Place.	MARRIAGE, Date and Place.	TO WHOM MARRIED.	REMARKS.
591	Henry Clay and S. C. B. Hartman.					
1131	Elizabeth Hartman.					
613	Benjamin Franklin and Jane Paincette Barber.					
1132	Maggie Barber,	Dec. 15, 1873.				
625	Samuel and Jane C. Kennedy Clark.					
1133	Mary Clark,				· · · · · ·	Belvidere, N. J.
626	Charles and Sarah Ann Kennedy Corse.					
1134	James Corse,					Lock Haven, Pa.
1135	Jennie Clark Corse.				· · · · · ·	
638½	Hewlett Jacob and Charlotte Rhodes Davis.					
1136	Charles Davis,		· · ·	· · ·	· · ·	Lock Haven, Pa.
1137	Gail Davis,		· · ·	· · ·	· · ·	Lock Haven, Pa.
1138	Louise Davis,		· · ·	· · ·	· · ·	Lock Haven, Pa.
1139	. . . Davis,		· · ·	· · ·	· · ·	Lock Haven, Pa.
1140	L. Davis,		· · ·	· · ·	· · ·	Lock Haven, Pa.
666	Chauncey and Emma S. Culbertson Ives.					
1141	Ellen Culbertson Ives,	Oct. 6, 1873.				
1142	Charlotte Brunnell Ives,	March 28, 1876.				
668	Daniel H. and Nannie Purviance Culbertson Wingert.					
1143	Margaret Kennedy Wingert	Jan. 26, 1879.				

No.	NAME.	BIRTH, DATE AND PLACE.	DEATH, DATE AND PLACE.	MARRIAGE, DATE AND PLACE.	TO WHOM MARRIED.	REMARKS.
669	James K. and Nannie P. Armstrong Culbertson.					
†1111	Edward Culbertson, . . .	. . . .	Died in infancy.			
685	Theodore and Alice Armstrong Chambers McGowan.					
1115	William Chambers McGowan	July 28, 1872.			. . .	Chambersburg, Pa.
1116	Bessie McGowan, . . .	August, 1874.			. . .	Chambersburg, Pa.
1117	Annie Thomson McGowan,	Dec. 30, 1878.			. . .	Chambersburg, Pa.
716	Child of Phineas Kennedy Reeves.					
1118	Arthur Kennedy Reeves, .	Oct. 27, 1880,			. . .	Bridgeton, N. J.
733	George Howard and Katherine North Greenleaf Duffield.					
†1149	George Greenleaf Duffield,	Feb. 3, 1878,	July 20, 1878,	. .	. . .	Princeton, N. J.
1150	Howard Leal Duffield,	June 27, 1879.	. . . . .		. . .	Princeton, N. J.
788	Frank L. and S. Augusta Heaton Daniels.					
1151	Ethyl Daniels, ...	Dec. 10, 1879.				
817	Byron and Amine Wilson Taylor.					
1152	James W. Taylor, ...	Jan. 23, 1859.				
†1153	Edgar A. Taylor, ...	Feb. 24, 1861.	August 3, 1863.			
818	William W. and Mahala Slabner Wilson.					
1154	Ida Pearl Wilson,	May 8, 1874.				

No.	NAME.	BIRTH. Date and Place.	DEATH. Date and Place.	MARRIAGE. Date and Place.	TO WHOM MARRIED.	REMARKS.
821	OVID O. and ABELLA GIBSON WILSON.					
1155	C. H. Wilson.	April 8, 1876.				
1156	Walter R. Wilson,	April 8, 1878.				
823	SILAS and ADA ABELL DAVIS.					
1157	Agnes Davis.					
1158	Roda Davis.					
824	A. and RODA ABELL MASON.					
1159	Lottie Mason.					
1160						
829	FRANK and ANNE ROGERS CHAMBERLAIN.					On page 47, where the Nos. 829, 830, and 831 appear, the name King is incorrectly printed for Chamberlain.
1161	Earl W. Chamberlain,	Sept. 2, 1874.				
1162	Ida Chamberlain,	Dec. 19, 1878.				
869	RICHARD H. and EMMA JANE BEAR BEAR.					
1163	Frederick Bear,	April 1867				
1164	Jessamine Bear,	1877.				
1165	Richard Bear,	1878.				
871	C. A. and MARY WILLA-MINA BEAR SHRIVER.					
1166	Alonzo Shriver.					
1167	Cora Shriver.					
1168	Estella Shriver.					
1169	Kennedy Shriver.					
873	BENJAMIN F. and JANE MAR-GARET BEAR THURBER.					
1170	William Leonard Thurber,	Aug. 14, 1874.				

No.	NAME	BIRTH, DATE AND PLACE	DEATH, DATE AND PLACE	MARRIAGE, DATE AND PLACE	TO WHOM MARRIED	REMARKS.
†1171	Julia Thurber, . . .	Sept. 8, 1876,	March, 1877.			
1172	Harry Albert Thurber, . .	May 15, 1879.				
884	Cyrus S. and Clarissa Jane Bates Bowman.					
1173	Ola B. Bowman, . . .	March 13, 1868,			. . .	Bryan, Ohio.
1174	Nina Bowman, . . .	April 11, 1870,			. . .	Bryan, Ohio.
1175	Harry Bowman, . . .	Jan. 25, 1872,			. . .	Bryan, Ohio.
1176	Ella Bowman, . . .	Oct. 20, 1874,			. . .	Bryan, Ohio.
1177	Dora Bowman, . . .	June 15, 1876.			. . .	Bryan, Ohio.
885	Horner and Frances Hoover Phillis.					
1178	Harry Phillis, . . .	July 4, 1878.			. . .	Kansas.
886	Curtis and Mary Phillis Beeciler.					
1179	Achasa Beeciler, . . .	1880.			. . .	A son. Kansas.
888	John W. and Jennie Logan Moorhead Watt.					
1180	Max Kennedy Moorhead Watt, . .	Feb. 14, 1879,			. . .	Pittsburgh, Pa.
1181	Mary Moorhead Watt, . .	1880,			. . .	Pittsburgh, Pa.
961	George N. and Elizabeth L. Stewart West.					
1182	Anna Edna West, . . .	Oct. 5, 1870,			. . .	Washington, D. C.
1183	George Stetson West, . .	June 6, 1872,			. . .	Washington, D. C.
1184	Bessie West, . . .	June 6, 1872,			. . .	Washington, D. C.
1185	Harry Stewart West, . .	Sept. 3, 1874,			. . .	Washington, D. C.
1186	Mabel E. West, . . .	March 3, 1877,			. . .	Washington, D. C.

HISTORICAL.

KENNEDY—Celtic, CEANNA-THIGHE—meaning, it is said, the head of a sept or clan. The family descend from the ancient Earls of Carrick, in Ayrshire, and seem to have changed their name from Carrick to Kennedy in the fourteenth century. The chief was Kennedy of Dunewe, afterwards Earl of Cassilis (now Marquis of Ailsa). In the fifteenth century the power of this great house, in the shires of Ayr and Galloway, was set forth in a popular rhyme:—

> "By Wigton and the town of Ayre,
> Port Patrick and the Cruives o' Cree,
> Nae man need think for to bide there,
> Unless he court wi' Kennedie."

The foregoing is from the "*Patronymica Britannica*," by Mark Anthony Lower. "Cruives is a trap made of sticks, placed in a river to catch salmon and other fish." Albert Edward, Prince of Wales, is the present Earl of Carrick. He has travelled on the Continent by that title.

The following is from Arthur's "*Etymological Dictionary of Family and Christian Names:*"—

"KENNEDY—from the Gallic or Celtic words Kean-na-ty—the head of the house, or chief of the clan. CEANNAIDE signifies also a shopkeeper, a merchant."

The following is from C. S. Sims's "*Scottish Surnames*," page 63:—

"KENNEDY, the chief of the clan. Duncan de Carrick, living in 1153, was father of Nichol de Carrick, whose son, Roland de Carrick, tem. Alexander III., took the name of Kennedy, and was the ancestor of the family."

A charter of Nigel, Earl of Carrick, to Roland de Carrick and his heirs, of the chieftainship of his clan; and the right of leading them, under the chief, was confirmed in 1241, and reconfirmed by Robert II. Roland de Carrick was killed in the Holy War; probably he commanded the military expedition organized in 1268, by Adam, Earl of Carrick, against the Saracens. Mention is made that a tract of land was confirmed to him by Alexander III., who reigned from 1249 to 1286.

Robert de Bruce, Lord of Annandale, was married, in 1271, to Martha Margaret, daughter of the Earl of Carrick, and his sole heiress; and in her own right, Countess of Carrick, and by virtue of her right, de Bruce became Earl of Carrick. She was the ward of Alexander III., and he was so much opposed to the marriage that he deprived her of her estate, but afterwards he restored it. Their eldest son, Robert the Bruce, was born March 21, 1272. By the resignation of his father he became Earl of Carrick in 1293. He was crowned King of Scotland, at Scone, March 27, 1306. He carried on an active war against England for twenty-three years. Amongst other adventures, in 1307 he attacked his patrimonial castle of Carrick, at midnight, and drove the English soldiers out of it. Finally, England, in the year 1328, renounced her claim to the crown of Scotland, and on the 9th of July, the following year, the Bruce died. His son David, in 1328, when only four years old, was married to Jane, sister of Edward of England. He ascended the throne as David II., on the death of his father, in 1329; crowned at Scone, November 14, 1331. After many vicissitudes, he died in 1371, without issue.

Walter Steward married Margery, King Robert the Bruce's only daughter by his first wife. Robert Steward, their son, to whom the crown was entailed, by authority of the Scotch Parliament, in default of male issue by David, was crowned King of Scotland in 1371. He was known as Robert II., and was the first of the Stuart dynasty; his son succeeded him as Robert III. This name was originally written Steward, then Stewart. Queen Mary, after her return from France, was the first to write it Stuart.

Edward Bruce, another son of Martha Margaret, Countess of Carrick, was crowned King of Ireland in 1316, and killed on the battle-field in 1318. All the other children of the countess, except Mary, were executed by the English government.

A charter of David II. to John MacKennedy (Mac signifies son of), the captain of Clan Muntercasduff, authorizes "James Kennedy, who had married Mary Stewart (the daughter of King Robert III., who was the second monarch of the Stuart dynasty), and heirs male, to exercise the captainship, head, and commandment of his kin."

Previous to the fourteenth century surnames were not known in Scotland. Individuals were distinguished by an affix to their Christian name, indicating some peculiarity of their personal appearance, their business, trade, district or clan to which they belonged. Roland de Carrick probably signifies Roland of the District or Earldom of Carrick. The hereditary title or office of Kennedy was conferred on him during the thirteenth century, by the highest lawful authority of the land.

The name of John MacKennedy merely signifies John the son of Kennedy. During the early part of the fourteenth century, the descendants of Roland de Carrick adopted Kennedy as a surname, consequently all the numerous Kennedys of the present day descended from the Ayrshire family, who are lawfully entitled to the name, are his lineal descendants. This explanation will make clear the apparent inconsistency between the quotations from Mark Anthony Lower and C. S. Sims.

We have not been able to trace the exact relationship between the Countess of Carrick, her son, King Robert the Bruce, and the Kennedys; we therefore have compiled the facts relating thereto, as they appear in Scotch history, and without comment will leave the readers free to form their own judgment.

The name of O'Cinnidh appears in Irish history during the tenth century. He was Regent of Munster. Anglicized Kennedy, it signifies a nation or kind. His descendants succeeded to the throne, and were very prominent people, but they all took different names, and the name of Kennedy, for a time, became extinct in Ireland; but after a lapse of several centuries it was revived. as a surname. As they do not seem to have been connected with the Ayrshire family of Kennedys, we dispose of the subject with this brief notice.

James Kennedy, Archbishop of St. Andrews, whose mother was the aunt of King James II. of Scotland, is said to have been one of the most powerful and influential statesmen of Scotland of his time. Through his influence Henry of England, after his misfortunes, was received and protected by Scotland.

For the purpose of refreshing the memory it seems proper that we should introduce, although in a very brief way, a few important facts connected with the Scotch history of the sixteenth century. in order to show the position of the Kennedy family during the religious and political trials of that period. The Kennedys early threw their influence in favor of the Reformed Religion. At first they were somewhat divided; but as early as 1538, Alexander Kennedy. of Ayr. a finely-educated young gentleman, only eighteen years old, a poet, was burned at the stake, in Glasgow, for a poetical satire against the Franciscan Friars.

John Knox was born 1505; he was educated for the priesthood; professed himself a Protestant in 1542. This same year the Scotch Parliament authorized the reading of the Scriptures in the vulgar languages. The Confession of Faith of the Reformers was adopted in 1560.

The Scotch Parliament abolished the Papal jurisdiction, and prohibited the celebration of the mass, August 24, 1560. The third violation of the law, in celebrating the mass, was punishable by death.

Gilbert Kennedy, Earl of Cassilis, was one of the ambassadors sent to negotiate the marriage of Queen Mary to the Dauphin of France. The earl died while in Paris.

Queen Mary returned to Scotland in 1561. very soon after the death of her first husband, the King of France. She was executed February 7, 1587. Jane Kennedy and Mistress Curle were the only two of her maids of honor who were permitted to attend the queen to the scaffold.

QUINTON KENNEDY.

Quinton Kennedy, the uncle of the Earl of Cassilis, and Abbot of Crossraguel, who is very highly spoken of for his intellectual and moral character, in 1559 challenged Wallock to a discussion on the Sacrifice of the Mass. The challenge was accepted. Kennedy claimed that they should use, as authority, the ancient doctors' interpretation of the Scriptures, which the other party would not agree to, and thus ended the matter.

On the 28th of September, 1562, a formal agreement was signed by John Knox and Quinton Kennedy, for a written argument on the Sacrifice of the Mass. The discussion was in the town of Mabole. In addition to the notaries to record the proceedings there were admitted, as spectators for each side, forty noblemen and persons of distinction. The place was not sufficient for the comfortable accommodation of so large a company. The argument, however, was continued for three days, but it proved uninteresting to the spectators, and, through the influence of the Earl of Cassilis, it was abandoned as being unprofitable. Each party claimed the victory, and each failed in accomplishing their expressed desire to have it renewed at a different time and place.

Quinton Kennedy died in August, 1564; and it is said that after his death he was canonized as a saint. His name, however, does not appear at Rome amongst the saints, but the subject of this debate is there canonized.

A SINGULAR INCIDENT, JUNE 26, 1629.

The lightning entered a room in Castle Kennedy, the seat of the Earl of Cassilis, in Ayrshire, where several children, with their dogs, were playing at the time; the dogs were killed, but the children escaped without injury.

THE KENNEDYS WERE LOWLANDERS.

None of the lowland clans had a distinctive tartan, and the kilts were not worn by the men; but they often clothed their children in this beautiful dress.

KENNEDYS IN THE SEVENTEENTH CENTURY.

The Kennedys, though Protestants, were not in favor of the high-handed political measures of the seventeenth century. They were opposed to the decapitation of King Charles I. (January 30, 1649), and they gave only a passive submission to the administration of Oliver Cromwell.

There was a joint Commission of Seven appointed by the Estates and Kirk of Scotland, who set sail on the 17th of March, 1649, for the Hague, to present to the Prince of Wales a proposition, that if he would sign the Covenant, and agree to adopt the Presbyterian form of worship, that Scotland would acknowledge him as their lawful sovereign. They arrived on the 26th of March, and on the 19th of May Charles declined to sign the document presented; but on his arrival in Scotland, on the 23d of June, and before he landed, he signed what is known as the Covenant.

The distinguished nobleman, John Kennedy, the Earl of Cassilis, who was also an influential ruling elder in the Presbyterian Church, was appointed by both parties, and, armed with his double commission, he was the acknowledged "chief person" in bringing about the restoration of King Charles II.

The Kennedys' uncompromising support of Presbyterianism, and love of law and order, rendered them liable to be crushed between the two conflicting powers of Charles II. and Cromwell. Some of them went to Holland, and many of them removed from Ayrshire to the North of Ireland, and from thence to America.

There was a commission appointed by Cromwell, in 1652, for the purpose of appraising the property of two hundred and sixty prominent Scots, residing in Ulster, Ireland, with the view of giving them a corresponding value in land at other parts of Ireland, to be occupied by them, and in this way to neutralize their influence. Amongst their names we find the following:—Quinton Kennedy, David Kennedy, Lieut. Col. Robert Kennedy, Anthony Kennedy, and Fergus Kennedy. This order was not executed, but we find that Lieut. Col. Robert Kennedy was removed the next year.

BATTLE OF BOTHWELL BRIDGE.

Sir Archibald Kennedy, Laird of Culzen, captain of the militia troops in 1685, was charged with great cruelty, in arresting and bringing to judgment the rebellious Covenanters, after their disastrous defeat at Bothwell bridge, in 1679.

CHAIN OF THE KENNEDYS FROM SCOTLAND TO IRELAND, AND THENCE TO AMERICA.

John Kennedy, sixth Earl of Cassilis, was one of the three Scotch noblemen appointed to act as lay assessors to the Westminster Assembly, in 1643. He never, however, attended. His brother, Col. Gilbert Kennedy, who was with Cromwell at the battle of Marston Moor, had two sons who were Presbyterian ministers—Thomas and Gilbert. Rev. Thomas Kennedy, the eldest, was chaplain to Gen. Munro, who came to Ireland with his army in 1642. Mr. Kennedy afterwards settled in Carland. He refused to conform—that is, to use the prescribed formula for public worship—and was imprisoned in Dungannon for several years, by the order of the Primate of Armagh. During his long imprisonment his wife was not allowed to see him, or even write to him. She, however, continued daily to bring him food and change of linen, which she gave to the jailer, to be handed to him. After the release of her husband, she learned from him that the jailer had appropriated her presents to his own use. Some years after this the jailer, being in want, applied to Mrs. Kennedy for food; instead of refusing him, she filled his bag with meal, saying, In this way I have my revenge. Mr. Kennedy's trials were so great that he thought at one time of removing to America, but his death, in 1714, ended all his troubles. Two of his sons, Thomas and John, were Presbyterian ministers.

It is believed that Robert and William Kennedy, the brothers who emigrated from Ireland and settled in Bucks County, Pennsylvania, in 1730, were the descendants of

Col. Gilbert Kennedy, probably his eldest son Thomas's sons or grandsons. We are led to believe that the founders of the family in America were influenced in the choice of their location, in order to enjoy the society of their cousin, Mrs. Catherine Kennedy Tennent, the wife of Rev. William Tennent, who had settled in Bucks County two years before their arrival.

REV. GILBERT KENNEDY.

The youngest son of Col. Gilbert Kennedy was ordained by the Presbyterian Church as a minister of Girvan, in Ayrshire, in 1651. He was ejected from the church in 1662, for nonconformity. He continued to preach in the glens by starlight, where the children of the neighborhood were brought to him to be baptized. He was compelled finally to flee from Scotland to Holland; from there he returned to Ireland in 1668, and settled in Dundonald, near Belfast, where he died, February 6, 1688, and was buried in the aisle of the church. He had a son named Gilbert, who was ordained a minister of Tullylish in 1704; also a daughter, Catherine, who was married May 15, 1702, to a student of theology, named William Tennent. Mr. Tennent was ordained a deacon of the Episcopal Church, July, 1704, and a priest, September 22, 1706. In 1716 Mr. Tennent left Ireland with his family for America. In 1718 he made a written application to the Presbyterian Synod of Philadelphia, stating his reasons for desiring to leave the Episcopal Church and to join the Presbyterian. The statement being satisfactory, he was received ; and for several years he preached in the neighborhood of Philadelphia and New York. In 1726 he was called to the Presbyterian church on the Neshaminy, Bucks County, Pennsylvania. In 1728 he built the celebrated Log College, on a tract of fifty acres of ground adjoining his house. This land was presented to him by his cousin, James Logan, secretary for William Penn. At this period this was the only place in America, west of the New England States, where a young man could receive a classical and theological education, to properly fit him for the ministry.

The General Assembly of the Presbyterian Church placed such value on the association that in 1811, when they were about to establish a more perfect system of education, many advocated placing the proposed new colleges on the same ground ; others advocated Chambersburg, Pennsylvania; but finally it was concluded to place them at Princeton, New Jersey.

The attentive reader will notice that the Kennedys were positive characters, and men of position and influence. There seems to have been a very close connection between them and the early Reformation in Scotland ; the Westminster Assembly ; the establishing of Presbyterianism, not only in the North of Ireland but also in America ; and up to the time of writing, 1880, the family have retained their loyalty to the Presbyterian Church, with few exceptions, and they generally the result of marriages with persons belonging to other denominations.

BIOGRAPHICAL.

(Letter A.)—ROBERT KENNEDY emigrated from the North of Ireland, in company with his younger brother William, and settled in Bucks County, Pennsylvania, in 1730. He died March 26, 1776, in his eighty-third year. His wife died June 3, 1773, aged 73. They are buried at the Stewart Burying Ground, near Bunker Hill, Tinicum Township, Bucks County.

They had one son, William Kennedy, a major in the Revolutionary Army. He was killed by some outlaws and Tories, named Doanes, in September, 1783, in the fortieth year of his age. He left five children.

Robert Kennedy to Jane McCalla,

- John McCalla Kennedy to Harriet Piper,
  - 4 children died without issue.
  - Henry Kennedy to Ellen Davis; 3 children.
  - Frank G. Kennedy to Margaret Lukens; 5 children.
  - Robert F. Kennedy to Rebecca Coombs; 2 children.
  - John M. Kennedy, Jr., to Carmita de Solms; 4 children.
  - Myra M. Kennedy to Thomas M. Adams; 5 children.
  - Ella L. Kennedy to William Elliott.
  - Emily B. Kennedy to Geo. H. McFadden; 2 children.
  - William M. Kennedy.
- William McCalla Kennedy, unmarried.
- Robert Kennedy, unmarried.
- Jane Kennedy, unmarried.
- Rebecca Kennedy to James M. Hirst,
  - Jane K. Hirst.
  - Mary Hirst.
  - Hannah Hirst to James Selfridge; 1 child.
  - Myra Hirst to James Gibbs; 5 children.
  - Virginia Hirst to George Pierie; 4 children.
- Myra Kennedy to Andrew C. Barclay.
  - William Barclay to Miss Heiskill.
  - Jane Barclay, unmarried.
  - John Barclay to Miss de Silver; 2 children.
  - Matilda Barclay, unmarried.
  - Emily Barclay, unmarried.
  - Charles Barclay to Miss Savage; 4 children.
  - Eliza Barclay to Mr. de Coursey; 3 children.

John Kennedy to Isabella Wigdon,

- William Kennedy,
  - Francine Kennedy.
  - John Kennedy.
- Elizabeth Kennedy to John M. Fenton,
  - H. Kennedy Fenton.
  - Hattie L. Fenton.
- Franklin Kennedy.
- Annabel Kennedy to George Mann; 1 child.

William Kennedy to Miss Ferris,

- Jas. Ferris Kennedy died in St. Clara, Cal.; left a large family.
- Martha Kennedy to Mr. Krotz; had 4 children.
- Wilmina Kennedy to Mr. Sexton; had 1 child.
- Anmira Kennedy.
- Mary Jane Kennedy.
- Louisa Kennedy.

Polly Kennedy and Nathan Shoemaker,

- Robert Shoemaker.
- Charles Shoemaker.
- William Shoemaker.

Jane Kennedy and Nathan Coalston.

JOHN McCALLA KENNEDY has been a very active and useful man. Early in life he engaged in a successful shipping business. For some years he has been an influential member of manufacturing and railroad corporations, and for many years a director of the Pennsylvania Railroad Company. Mr. Kennedy has commanded the respect of the community, and his prolonged life has been rewarded by the accumulation of a sufficiency of this world's goods to relieve him, in his old age, from the cares of a continued business life. His large family of children reside in or near Philadelphia, and occupy useful and respectable positions in society.

(No. 1.)—WILLIAM KENNEDY was born in Londonderry, Ireland, not far from Belfast, in 1695. He married Miss Mary Henderson; she was sometimes called by the synonymous Scotch name, Marian.

Their first son, Thomas, was about a year old when Mr. Kennedy removed his family from Ireland, in 1730, and, in connection with his older brother, Robert, settled in Bucks County, Pennsylvania, where he resided until the time of his death, in 1777; his remains are buried in this county. The names of their children can be found on the chart.

The name of Henderson frequently appears in Scotch history. A man by the name of Henderson read prayers, from the formula written by John Knox, at the High Church of St. Giles, at eight o'clock in the morning of the Sabbath on which the unfortunate attempt was made, a few hours thereafter, in the same church, to introduce the prescribed formula for public worship, that brought on the celebrated riot that, in its results, proved so unfortunate for the Stuart dynasty.

Rev. Alexander Henderson was the leading delegate from Scotland to the Westminster Assembly, and the principal author of the Assembly's Catechism.

(No. 3.)—JAMES KENNEDY, son of William and Mary, or Marian Kennedy, as she was sometimes called, was born in Bucks County, Pennsylvania, in 1730, probably very soon after his parents arrived in America. He was married in 1761 to Jane Maxwell, daughter of John Maxwell, and sister of Gen. Maxwell of the Revolutionary Army. At the time of their marriage she was in her nineteenth year. She died September 7, 1784, and was buried in Bucks County. The names of their twelve children are on the connected chart. Afterwards, Mr. Kennedy married Miss Jane Macalla; there was not any issue by this marriage, and they both died October, 1799, and were buried in the same grave, at Pequea, about six miles from the Gap, Lancaster County, Pennsylvania. In 1788 Mr. Kennedy purchased a farm of 480 acres, at the Gap, Lancaster County. The title to this property has passed by bequest, and at the time of writing, 1880, part of it is owned and cultivated by his grandson, Sylvester Kennedy; the balance of it is owned by his great-great-granddaughter, Mrs. Emma Kennedy Lewis, of Brooklyn, New York. This farm will still be favorably noticed by the traveller on the Pennsylvania Railroad, when at a point near the west entrance of the Gap, and opposite Belle Vue Presbyterian Church, looking north.

The beautiful surroundings, for a distance of five miles, are brought directly in view, and richly reward the traveller's observation. Small farms of one hundred acres, in high state of cultivation, dotted with handsome dwellings, present the appearance of adorned pleasure grounds surrounding luxuriant country seats.

Mr. Kennedy brought up all of his children in the Presbyterian faith. It was the custom for good people, in those days, to consecrate one of their sons to the service of the Lord; with this object in view he gave his son Robert the best classical education that the country at that time would admit of, and in due time he entered the ministry. An account of his useful life can be found in another part of this book.

(No. 11.)—WILLIAM KENNEDY, son of James and Jane Maxwell Kennedy, was born in 1766. He died at Easton, Pennsylvania, in 1850. On January 28, 1798, he married Sarah Stewart; they had eight children. (See chart.)

When only fifteen years old, Mr. Kennedy offered his services to the Continental Government, and served as an aid to his uncle, Gen. Maxwell. In politics he was a Democrat, and represented the counties of Sussex and Warren in the Legislature of New Jersey for several successive sessions, presiding with honor and dignity over the upper house. In the same counties he served for many years as judge of the courts. A man of much natural ability, he possessed, throughout his long course of public life, a wide influence in that section of the State.

His lively sympathy led him to take an active part in relieving the sufferings occasioned by the war of 1812.

In religion a Presbyterian, he was an elder in the church at Greenwich.

(No. 17.)—ROBERT KENNEDY, son of James and Jane Maxwell Kennedy, was born at the Gap, Lancaster County, Pennsylvania, July 4, 1778. He died at the Welsh Run, Franklin County, October 31, 1843, and was buried at the Red Church, Greencastle.

Mr. Kennedy received his elementary and classical education at a school not far from his father's, taught by Mr. Grier; his collegiate course he received at Dickinson College, Carlisle, where he graduated with honor, September 20, 1797. He made a profession of religion at the Pequea Presbyterian Church, soon after leaving college. He commenced the study of theology with the Rev. Nathaniel Sample, then pastor of Lancaster and Middle Octorara Presbyterian Churches, on the 20th of August, 1799. He was licensed to preach by the New Castle Presbytery, and appointed to supply the pulpit at Octorara half of his time. On the 9th of October, 1802, he accepted a call to East and Lower West Conococheague Presbyterian Churches, since known as Greencastle and Welsh Run; and on the 13th of August, 1803, he was ordained. He continued to preach here until the 9th of April, 1816, when he removed to Cumberland, Maryland, to take charge of a church and a classical seminary. He remained here until 1825, when he returned to his farm at the Welsh Run. He taught a classical school at Mercersburg, and preached half of his time at the Welsh Run, and the other half at some of the surrounding churches.

Mr. Kennedy was a very industrious, practical man, and supplemented his salary with the proceeds of his school, and his farm of about 400 acres of rich land. He was married February 17, 1801, to Jane Herron, daughter of John Herron, and sister of the late Rev. Francis Herron, D.D., of Pittsburg. She died May 31, 1803. On June 5, 1806, he was married to Mary Davidson. daughter of Elias and Agnes McDowell Davidson, of Greencastle. Miss Davidson was born August 6, 1785, and died March 14, 1845. The names of their children are on the chart.

Mr. Kennedy was a sound theologian, and was ranked as a good preacher by the competent judges of Carlisle Presbytery. He was a fine classical scholar. He wrote with good taste, and expressed his views with great clearness.

The difficulties in the Presbyterian Church commenced in Carlisle Presbytery. Mr. Kennedy was sorely vexed at the approaching troubles, and threw himself into the breach, and used all his influence and power to prevent the division of the church. At the meeting of the Synod of Philadelphia, at Gettysburg, in 1834 (see October number, 1860, of Presbyterian Quarterly Review, published in Philadelphia; also, Men of Mark of Cumberland Valley), he made a speech in opposition to the Act and Testimony, which was very much admired for its condensed wit, argument, and persuasion; but the Presbyterian ship had drifted too far into the rapids to prevent her plunging over the falls. It is only necessary to add the almost-prophetic extract of a document signed by Mr. Kennedy:—"We cannot but hope that the time will come when we will again be united on the basis of our excellent Constitution." (See Harrisburg Presbytery, Pastoral Letter. 1840.) A hope which was fulfilled about thirty years after his death.

Mr. Kennedy's memory was held in such esteem at the Welsh Run that the trustees have had the chartered name of the church changed to the Robert Kennedy Memorial Presbyterian Church.

Mr. Kennedy was a Federalist, afterwards a Whig.

(No. 89.)—JAMES KENNEDY MOORHEAD, son of William and Elizabeth Kennedy Young Moorhead, was born September 7, 1806, in Halifax Township, Dauphin County, Pennsylvania.

At the age of sixteen he was apprenticed to William Linville, of Lancaster County, to learn the art of tanning.

In 1827 he engaged as a contractor on the Susquehanna and Juniata Divisions of the Pennsylvania Canal. in which business he continued until 1838.

About this time he became interested in the Pioneer Packet Line, between Philadelphia and Pittsburgh, which rendered his removal to the latter place necessary.

In 1839 he was appointed, by President Van Buren. Postmaster at Pittsburgh.

In 1846 he was elected President of the Monongahela Navigation Company, which, under his administration, has been a continuous success from its organization. He has been very extensively engaged in successful manufacturing enterprises in Pittsburgh. Mr. Moorhead has also held the position of president in several railroad and telegraph enterprises.

In 1858 he was elected a Representative to Congress from the Pittsburgh District, and was re-elected for four successive terms. At this most critical period of the nation's history he proved himself one of the most active, able, and influential supporters of the government.

Mr. Moorhead has made liberal use of his large fortune in support of religious and charitable institutions in Pittsburgh, and is widely known and much respected.

In 1830 he married Jane Logan, of Lancaster County. They have had eight children. (See chart.)

Mr. and Mrs. Moorhead celebrated their Golden Wedding. December 17, 1879, surrounded by their children, grandchildren, and one great-grandchild, and many relatives and friends. Mr. Moorhead is a leading member in the Presbyterian Church.

Since its organization he has been an influential member of the Republican Party.

(No. 90.)—JOEL BARLOW MOORHEAD, son of William Moorhead and Elizabeth Kennedy Young Moorhead, was born at Moorhead's Ferry, Dauphin County, Pennsylvania, April 13, 1813. He was married February 7, 1837, to Elizabeth Hirons, daughter of John Hirons, of Wilmington, Delaware. Their children's names are on the connected chart. Mr. Moorhead was early engaged in the construction of Pennsylvania State internal improvements, and for several years was State Manager of the Columbia Railroad, owned by the State. He also took a very active part in the construction of the Philadelphia and Erie Railroad, the Schuylkill Navigation Company, Monongahela Navigation Company, internal improvements of the State of Kentucky, and the local railroad system of the District of Columbia, in all of which he acquitted himself with credit and to the entire satisfaction of those with whom he was associated. For several years Mr. Moorhead has been very extensively and successfully engaged in the mining and manufacturing of iron in its crude state. He is also connected with a great many financial, charitable, and benevolent institutions. Mr. Moorhead, early in life, acted with the Democratic Party. About the time the attempt was made to introduce slavery into Kansas he abandoned the party, and since has been an active Republican. He was brought up in the Methodist faith. His wife was a Quaker, and, by mutual agreement, they have connected themselves with the Episcopal Church, and have brought up all their children according to the order of that faith. Mr. Moorhead is a large, fine-looking man, very frank in his manner, and unostentatious. He has led a very active life, and always enjoyed the confidence and respect of the community. Since his marriage he has resided in or near Philadelphia.

(No. 91.)—WILLIAM GARRAWAY MOORHEAD, son of William and Elizabeth Kennedy Young Moorhead, was born July 7, 1811, at Moorhead's Ferry, Dauphin County, Pennsylvania. Mr. Moorhead's business life commenced very early. At the age of seventeen he was appointed to important work in connection with the Juniata Canal, and held other State appointments, in connection with railroads, while still very young.

6

In 1834 he removed to Sandusky, Ohio, and engaged in mercantile pursuits, in partnership with his brother, James Kennedy Moorhead. While residing in Sandusky he married Sarah Cooke, the only daughter of the Hon. Elewtheros Cooke, a distinguished lawyer and member of Congress. The names of their four children are on the chart. Mrs. Sarah Cooke Moorhead died in Philadelphia. Afterwards Mr. Moorhead married Mrs. Cornelia Badger.

Mercantile life not being congenial to Mr. Moorhead, he very soon returned to Pennsylvania, and was identified with many of the public works then in progress, and gave valuable aid in procuring funds for various railroads and canals then in course of construction.

In 1846 Mr. Moorhead was appointed by President Polk, and confirmed by the Senate, Consul of the United States to Valparaiso, Chili; and, in addition, for several years the duties of Minister from the United States were performed by him. The following year he was appointed purchasing agent for the United States squadron in the Pacific. It was during this period that gold was discovered in California, and before leaving Chili Mr. Moorhead organized the firm of Moorhead, Whitehead & Waddington, who made large contracts with the millers of Chili for supplying flour to California. The operations of this firm were very large, the proceeds from the sales of flour, during the fifteen months of the firm's business, aggregating over $5,000,000. On his return to the United States he re-embarked in the construction of public works. He was elected President of the Philadelphia and Erie Railroad Company, and was instrumental in its successful completion.

In 1861 he formed a partnership with his brother-in-law, Jay Cooke, under the firm name of Jay Cooke & Co., and engaged in a general banking business. The firm was very successful, and established branches in Washington, New York city, and London. At this period the government had exhausted its resources. Jay Cooke and Wm. G. Moorhead advanced the idea to their personal friend, the Secretary of the Treasury, S. P. Chase, that the wealth of the nation was really in the hands of the people, and that the money could be borrowed from them. Jay Cooke & Co. acted as the agents of the United States Government; and it was at their suggestion, and through their instrumentality, aided by the press, that the government loan was speedily popularized, and placed on sale in every important town in the country. There can be no doubt but that Jay Cooke and Wm. G. Moorhead, in thus aiding the government, were important factors in the successful termination of the Rebellion.

In 1873, when the unexpected crash overwhelmed our country, Jay Cooke & Co. were unprepared for it; having advanced millions of dollars to the Northern Pacific Railroad Company, and having made large investments in railroad securities, which were unavailable at the time, the firm, so prosperous but a short time previous, was obliged to succumb.

Mr. Moorhead has always been an active and benevolent man, and enjoys the esteem of those who know him. He is now (1880) an elder in the Presbyterian Church in West Philadelphia, and is active in church work.

In politics he has always been a conservative Democrat.

For a more minute account of Mr. Moorhead's very active life the reader is referred to the Biographical Encyclopedia of Pennsylvania.

(No. 99.)—JOHN HERRON KENNEDY, son of Rev. Robert and Jane Herron Kennedy, was born at Herron's Run, near Shippensburg, Pennsylvania, November 11, 1801. He died at Canonsburg, December 15, 1840. Was married in Philadelphia, February 15, 1827, to Harriet McCalmont. Their issue are named on the chart.

Mr. Kennedy received his elementary and classical education under his father's care. He graduated, with honor, at Jefferson College, Canonsburg, in May, 1820. He studied theology at Princeton Seminary, and in October, 1822, was licensed by Carlisle Presbytery to preach; and in November, 1825, he was ordained and installed pastor of the Sixth Presbyterian Church of Philadelphia. He resigned this charge December, 1829. Previous to his settlement in this church he had been appointed chaplain to the government ship Brandywine, selected by the government to carry Gen. Lafayette back to France; this appointment, however, failed to reach him until after his installation. On the 11th of March, 1830, he received a call from the Presbyterian Church of "Center," and in connection therewith the appointment of Professor of Mathematics in Jefferson College.

Rev. Matthew Brown, D.D., says of him: "That as an instructor he was discriminating, accurate, and lucid in his illustrations; as a member of the faculty he was energetic, fearless, and ready to share the responsibility of a disciplined government; as a preacher he was instructive, solemn, searchable and forcible; as a pastor he was laborious and faithful; as a writer he was characteristically lucid, simple and concise."

Mr. Kennedy was a Whig. (See Men of Mark of Cumberland Valley.)

(No. 103.)—JAMES MAXWELL KENNEDY, son of Rev. Robert and Mary Davidson Kennedy, was born at Welsh Run, Franklin County, Pennsylvania, February 24, 1809. He died at Philadelphia, March 9, 1848. Was married in Philadelphia, November 23, 1836, to Sibilla Stone Morris, daughter of Evan Morris, of Chester County. Their children's names are on the chart.

Mr. Kennedy received his education at his father's classical academy at Cumberland, Maryland. Soon after his arrival at manhood he repaired to Philadelphia, to engage in the wholesale dry goods business, at first as clerk, but after two years he commenced business for himself, as the head of the following successful firms, as they from time to time changed:—Kennedy, Bowman & Co., Kennedy, Julian & Co., and James M. Kennedy & Co.

Mr. Kennedy was a gentleman of fine personal appearance and elegant manners. He was very resolute and brave. In religion a Presbyterian; in politics a Whig.

(No. 107.)—ELIAS DAVIDSON KENNEDY, son of the Rev. Robert and Mary Davidson Kennedy, was born the 27th of December, 1819, at Cumberland, Maryland. Six years afterwards his father removed to Welsh Run, Franklin County, Pennsylvania. Elias Davidson lived with his parents until 1839, when he came to Philadelphia, to enter the wholesale dry goods store of his brother, James M. Kennedy; here he remained, part of the time as clerk and afterward as a partner, until his brother's death,

March 9, 1848. In December of that year he formed a partnership with another brother, under the name "E. D. & W. T. Kennedy." The new firm purchased a stock of general dry goods, &c., and determined to start for California, W. T. Kennedy going overland, in the company of his cousin, Thomas B. Kennedy, and Elias Davidson Kennedy taking passage, with the stock of merchandise, in the "Levant," from Philadelphia, via Cape Horn. After a tedious and perilous voyage of seven months, the "Levant" anchored off San Francisco, and early the next morning Mr. Kennedy was met by his brother, who had been in California some weeks, and was dismayed and discouraged at their prospects.

The two brothers decided that Sacramento was the most available place to dispose of their merchandise, and from the day of their arrival in that city they did a large and profitable business. Twice was their house destroyed—once by fire and once by flood —but notwithstanding these, and many drawbacks, their business continued to prosper. In 1851 they added banking to their general business. Mr. Kennedy made in all four distinct trips to California.

On the 20th of April, 1854, he married Miss Agnes Shields Clarke, only daughter of Thomas Shields and Eliza Thaw Clarke. Mr. Clarke was a prominent shipping merchant of Pittsburgh, Pennsylvania, and highly esteemed. Immediately after their marriage they left for a tour in Europe. Some time after their return, accompanied by his wife, he went to California to settle the estate of his brother, William T. Kennedy, who died in Philadelphia, December 8, 1855. While in California their daughter Alice was born. In the fall of 1857 they returned to Philadelphia, where they have since resided. They have had two daughters and five sons. (See chart.)

It was Mr. Elias Davidson Kennedy who first proposed to build a church, and afterward furnished the means for its erection, at Welsh Run, Franklin County, Pennsylvania, in memory of his father's years of labor as pastor of the congregation centering around that place. This building was completed about 1870, and stands on or near the site of the old church, built in 1760, in which his father had preached so many years. It is a neat and tasteful edifice, and is called the "Robert Kennedy Memorial Presbyterian Church."

Whilst Mr. Kennedy partakes of that nervous, quick temperament and positive manner peculiar to the Kennedys, he in appearance resembles the Davidsons; is tall and well proportioned, with dark complexion, black eyes, black hair and whiskers.

In business Mr. Kennedy was a man of sagacity and integrity, and success has attended all his undertakings. In religion he is a Presbyterian, and in politics a Republican.—(*Contributed by* T. B. K.)

(No. 259.)—Thomas B. Kennedy was born August 1, 1827, in Warren County, New Jersey. His father, Hon. James J. Kennedy, removed to Chambersburg, Pennsylvania, in 1839. Mr. Kennedy entered the sophomore class of Marshall College at fourteen, and graduated with honor in 1844. He read law with the Hon. Alexander Thompson, of Chambersburg, and was admitted to the Franklin County bar in 1848. The next year he crossed the plains as the leader of a company bound for California.

In 1851 he returned to Chambersburg and commenced the practice of law. He served one term as District Attorney. with general approbation. He afterwards went into partnership with the Hon. James Nill. The business of the firm rapidly increased, so that upon the elevation of Judge Nill to the bench of the district, in 1862, his partner found himself in control of the largest and most lucrative practice at the bar, which he has steadily maintained. Mr. Kennedy has freely used the income from his large estate in sustaining Wilsons College, and all the religious and benevolent institutions of the place. He was married April 22, 1856, to Ariana Stuart Riddle. Soon after marriage they spent a year travelling in Europe. They have had six children. (See chart.) Mr. Kennedy has been President of the Cumberland Valley Railroad and its connections for some years. The present success of the road is principally the result of his good judgment and untiring industry.

Mr. Kennedy is a gentleman of fine personal appearance, with black eyes, black hair and whiskers. He is a Presbyterian ; in politics a Democrat.

(No. 283.)—REV. WILLIAM HENRY GREEN, D.D., LL.D., son of George and Sallie Kennedy Green. was born at Groveville, near Bordentown, New Jersey, on the 27th of January, 1825. He graduated at Lafayette College, Easton, Pennsylvania, 1840, where he remained a short time as tutor. He studied theology in Princeton, and, upon the completion of his course, in 1846, he was made assistant teacher of Hebrew. After remaining three years in this capacity, during a portion of which he supplied successively the pulpits of the First and Second Churches in Princeton, he became the pastor of the Central Church, in Philadelphia. In 1851 he was elected Professor of Oriental and Biblical Literature in the Theological Seminary at Princeton, as successor of Dr. J. Addison Alexander. In 1859 the title of the Professorship was changed to that of Oriental and Old Testament Literature. In 1861 he published a Grammar of the Hebrew Language ; in 1863 a Hebrew Chrestomathy ; in 1866 an Elementary Hebrew Grammar ; in 1863 the Pentateuch Vindicated from the Aspersions of Bishop Colenso ; in 1870 he translated Zoechler's Commentary on the Song of Solomon ; he also published a Commentary on the Book of Job. His publications are too numerous here to mention, and the reader is referred to the Index Volume of the Princeton Review, page 185. At the time of writing (1880) Doctor Green is engaged with the Bible Revision Committee, composed of fifty-two eminent English and twenty-seven equally distinguished American divines, of different denominations. in translating the Bible from the original tongues into the English language. He is chairman of the Old Testament Committee.

Doctor Green was married June 24, 1852, to Mary Elizabeth Caldwell, daughter of Stephen and Elizabeth Caldwell, of Philadelphia. She died March 29, 1854, without issue. He was again married April 28, 1858, to Elizabeth Hays. daughter of Doctor Samuel and Eliza Keen Hays. They have had two children. (See chart.)

Doctor Green is a large man, fully six feet high, with a good physical constitution, and can bear an immense amount of professional work. He is a thorough Calvinistic Presbyterian in faith, and Republican in politics. He stands very high as a classical and theological scholar, and is ranked as a good preacher by the most competent judges.

(No. 505.)—REV. SYLVESTER F. SCOVEL, son of the Rev. Sylvester Scovel, D.D., President of Hanover College, was born at Harrison, Ohio, December 29, 1835; graduated at Hanover College in 1853, and immediately commenced the study of theology; was licensed to preach on the 7th of April, 1857, three months after attaining majority; was ordained and installed pastor of the Presbyterian Church of Jeffersonville, Indiana, October 28, 1857; accepted a call to Springfield, Ohio, January 7, 1861; accepted a call to the First Presbyterian Church of Pittsburgh, Pennsylvania, January, 1866.

A man of scholarly tastes and attainments; an able preacher and a faithful pastor; a public-spirited citizen; an accurate thinker and writer, he was appointed to read one of the essays before the General Presbyterian Council, which met in Philadelphia, September, 1880.

Mr. Scovel was married, October 6, 1857, to Miss Caroline Woodruff, daughter of C. Woodruff, formerly of Newark, New Jersey. The names of their children can be found on the foregoing chart.

RESTATEMENT OF No. 7.

The history of the descendants of Col. Arthur and Mary Kennedy Erwin was furnished by a very intelligent member of that connection. The author, relying upon the correctness of this report, was under the impression that the family was nearly extinct; but soon after "The Kennedy Family" had been published, it was apparent that this report included only the third generation, numbering 29 persons, whereas the aggregate number of their descendants, to this time, amounts to 295. It was evident that this very meagre account would leave a wrong impression, and it was thought best to give the following brief statement of the main facts :—

Col. Arthur Erwin and his second wife, Mary Kennedy, were married in 1768 or 1769. She died July 29, 1817. Col. Erwin was a patriotic and very prominent man of his day. As early as December 17, 1776, he was ordered by George Washington to march his regiment to Philadelphia and to report for duty to General Israel Putnam. The original order is now in the hands of Henry N. Paul, Esq., of Philadelphia. The boats used by the Revolutionary army to cross the Delaware river below Frenchtown were built by Col. Erwin. He was assassinated by a squatter while temporarily at the house of Daniel McDuffy, at Tioga Point, Luzerne County, Pennsylvania, on the 9th of June, 1791. At the time of his death he resided at Erwinna, Tinicum township, Bucks County, Pennsylvania, and was the richest man in that county. He owned in the township over two thousand acres of the most valuable land; also in Luzerne County, Pennsylvania, between four thousand and five thousand acres; also in Steuben County, New York, thirty thousand acres, on which latter have since been built the following towns :—Erwin, Painted Post, Cooper, Canisteo and Hornell-ville. His numerous descendants are cultured and influential, enjoying the advantages of wealth, and worthily proud of their ancestry. The following well-known names are included in the present generation :—The Pauls of Belvidere, New Jersey; Randolphs of Easton, Pennsylvania; Erwins, Coopers, Hickmans, Townsends, Stevens, Morses, Peases, and many others living on or near the patrimonial domains in Steuben County, New York, and other places.

www.ingramcontent.com/pod-product-compliance
Lightning Source LLC
Chambersburg PA
CBHW020308090426
42735CB00009B/1272